JACKSON
AND THE
PREACHERS

JOHN W. SCHILDT

McClain Printing Company
Parsons, West Virginia 26287
www.mcclainprinting.com
2004

International Standard Book Number 0-87012-445-5
Library of Congress Control Number 82-80743
Printed in the United States of America
Copyright © 1982 by McClain Printing Company
Parsons, WV
All Rights Reserved
2004

First Printing 1982
Second Printing 1992
Third Printing 1998
Fourth Printing 2004

McClain Printing Company
Parsons, West Virginia 26287
www.mcclainprinting.com
2004

This book is dedicated to the memory of the Reverend John W. Fisher, D.D., and the Reverend Harry C. Kottler, boyhood pastors of the author.

"Among the great gifts that God has given to men is the gift of men; and among all the gifts with which God has enriched His church, one of the greatest has been the gift of consecrated men, for they are the instrumentalities by which the church has been moulded and prospered in all the generations of the world."

These words were spoken by Dr. Moses Drury Hoge at the death of a friend. However, they apply to all the *PREACHERS JACKSON KNEW.*

PREACHERS JACKSON KNEW

ILLUSTRATIONS

PREFACE

Most people are aware of the relationship between Stonewall Jackson and Robert E. Lee, and a whole host of military figures. However, the last twelve years of his life were shaped by his close association with several Presbyterian preachers.

Rev. George Junkin was his first father-in-law. On the eve of the Civil War he thought Tom was "a very brave man, but a lunatic."

Dr. William S. White, his pastor in Lexington, was regarded by Jackson as his spiritual general and teacher. White visited Jackson in camp and conducted his funeral service.

To Rev. James Graham, he entrusted the care of his wife Anna in the winter of 1862. She regarded her stay in the manse in Winchester as some of the brightest moments of her life.

Dr. Moses Hoge was given a pass to travel at will in Jackson's army. Jackson urged him to go to Europe to get Bibles for the soldiers.

R. L. Dabney was Jackson's chief of staff for a time. He made a deep impression on the men by wearing a Prince Albert frock coat and a tall hat.

Beverly Lacy conducted the big revival in Fredericksburg in the winter of 1863, and was chaplain of the Second Corps. He conducted prayer meetings for Jackson.

Young James P. Smith was called to serve on Jackson's staff in Frederick. He was with his commander until the very end, and has left a tremendous account of the last days of Jackson's life. After the war he became an outstanding minister in Fredericksburg.

These are *Jackson's preacher friends,* the men you will meet in the pages of this book.

John W. Schildt

Chewsville, Maryland
February 6, 1981

WITH GRATITUDE

. . . to Rev. Foster Couchman, Mr. Ben Ritter, and Dr. James Miller, the Frederick County, Virginia, Historical Society, and the Handley Library for their assistance in researching material on Dr. James Graham, the Kent Street Church, and Jackson's stay in Winchester.

Mrs. Julia Smith Martin of the Public Information Office at the Virginia Military Institute, was of great help in supplying material about Jackson's home life, teaching career, and involvement in Lexington.

Dr. James Robertson, Robert Krick, and Lowell Reidenbaugh, all great Jackson scholars, came to the author's aid many times, and gave leads, insights, and biographical articles on the preachers.

Dr. Ruth See of the Presbyterian Historical Foundation in Montreat, North Carolina, provided ministerial records of the pastors, and biographical sketches.

The Union Theological Seminary Library in Richmond furnished the writer with books, biographies, and other articles about *the preachers Jackson knew.*

Likewise, the Presbyterian Churches in Fredericksburg, Lexington, Frederick, and Second Street in Richmond, along with the Presbyterian Church in Charles Town shared their records and church histories. All of the above played a role in bringing *Jackson's preachers* to you. For this we extend our sincere gratitude.

I

J. WILLIAM JONES

"No man lives or dies unto himself." We are the product of our environment and our times. Parents, family values, childhood friends and teachers all play a part in our growth and development. Likewise, we are influenced by the works of the artists and scientists, those who write poetry, and those who sing.

An individual is touched by those who write, and by the conversations he hears and shares in. God-given gifts, and human gifts inspire us and help us. The example and friendship of others also plays an important role. We are touched by sermons, silence, prayers, tears, rebukes, good, and evil. And our lives are touched by churches and by preachers.

Thomas Jonathan Jackson is known primarily for his ability "to move at an early hour," in his efforts to "divide and conquer" his enemy. However, he was a very religious man. He could also say, "I am a part of all whom I've ever met or known." During his two-year career as one of America's greatest military leaders, he touched and influenced many preachers, and they in turn touched and inspired him. This is the story of some of the *preachers Jackson knew.* We begin with the story of J. William Jones.

Jones was at Harpers Ferry in the spring of 1861. He, along with many other soldiers, asked the question, "Who is this Colonel Jackson who has been sent to command us?" They soon learned the answer. In forty-eight hours "we felt his strong hand, recognized the differences between him and certain militia officers who had previously had charge of the post, and realized that we were now under the command of a real soldier and a rigid disciplinarian."

Jones saw him frequently at Harpers Ferry; and "as a high private in the rear rank' of the Thirteenth Virginia Regiment it was sometimes my duty to pace the sentinel's beat in front of his headquarters."

J. William Jones

John William Jones was born September 25, 1836, in Louisa County, Virginia. He was the son of Colonel Francis

W. Jones and Anne Pendleton. After spending a year at the University of Virginia, Jones made the decision to enter the ministry. He was ordained on the eve of the Civil War as he graduated from the Southern Baptist Theological Seminary in Louisville. Later that year he married Judith Page Helm of Nelson County, Virginia. He was appointed to the mission field, and scheduled to go to China, but the impending war prevented his leaving.[1]

On June 8, 1861, Jones enlisted in Company D of the Thirteenth Virginia. The unit was known as the "Louisa Blues." A. P. Hill was the commanding officer. Four months later, Jones was named chaplain of the regiment. Jackson did not want the chaplains to go home. He felt they should share the plight of the men in the ranks. Jones did this to the hilt. He served throughout the war, being absent from the army but for two weeks in December of 1861. Jed Hotchkiss, Jackson's map maker, stated that Jones "shared the sufferings and privations and the risks of battle with the soldiers, ministered to them in hospitals, encouraged them in the performance of arduous duty, and was particularly effective in these famous revivals, which resulted in the religious profession of over fifteen thousand of Lee's veterans."

Like Jackson, Jones was a man of great energy, and like Dabney, he wrote many letters. During one twelve-month period, Jones preached 161 sermons and baptized 222 soldiers. He wrote constantly for the *Religious Herald,* based in Richmond. He wrote under the pen name of "Occasional." He was, in the words of Dr. James Robertson, "the most readable and reliable writer among Confederate Chaplains." Jones was also the key man in getting Baptist ministers into the army as chaplains. On the other hand, if he felt a man was unfit, he could say "no" to his entrance.

Jones met and knew Jackson as we shall see, but perhaps not as closely as some of the other preachers listed in this book. He was with A. P. Hill's command, and attached to Jackson corps from the fall of 1862 until the spring of 1863. He talked with Jackson often at Moss Neck and at Yerby's near Fredericksburg. However, to a larger degree, especially after Jackson's death, he was to assume the role of leadership in Hill's Third Corps, held by Lacy with Jackson in the Second. As the war went on, Jones was like "a missionary chaplain or chief of chaplains in the Third Corps of the Army of Northern Virginia.

J. William Jones was still a young man when hostilities ceased. He turned twenty-nine in the autumn of 1865, and accepted the pastorate of the Baptist Church in Lexington. He and Robert E. Lee arrived about the same time. The two became very close, and in addition to his pastoral work, Jones became chaplain of Washington College.

"Appomattox was not the end" for the Army of Northern Virginia. "Rather, it was the beginning of a proud army's march into history." Although the war had been lost, the veterans were proud to say they had served with Lee and Jackson. They were as proud as those of our day were of having served with Patton, Bradley, or MacArthur. Sandie Pendleton and others had stated during the war that one of the great legacies they would have to hand down to their children was the fact that they had served with Stonewall Jackson, and had been a part of the Second Corps. Other men echoed these feelings.

On November 3, 1870, a large number of Confederate veterans gathered in Richmond. From the gathering came the Army of Northern Virginia Association. The main objectives were "the preservation of the friendships that were formed in the army, the perpetuation of its fame, and the vindication of its achievements." Chapters were formed, and yearly meetings held.

The following year, Jones moved to Richmond, and served in various capacities with his denomination. He was an agent for the Southern Baptist Seminary, superintendent of the Virginia Baptist Sunday School program, and various other duties. He was well placed to be a part of the Army of Northern Virginia Association.

In 1878, the association voted to "publish a volume containing the major addresses and other important data presented at its annual gatherings." There was no major surprise when J. William Jones was selected. Dr. Robert-

4

son calls him "the most prolific of all the early Confederate historians."

Most of the *preachers Jackson knew* wrote books or were into literary pursuits. Jones, with his letters to Richmond during the war, and with all that he did later was the most outstanding.

Following the death of General Lee, the family asked Jones to prepare an official biography. This resulted in the preacher's first book, *Personal Reminiscences, Anecdotes, and Letters of Gen. Robert E. Lee.* This was published in 1874. Like many authors, this was the clergyman's first book, and his poorest. He picked up style in the next books.

Next came *Army of Northern Virginia Memorial Volume,*[2] (Richmond, 1880). This was followed by his classic, *Christ in Camp: Or Religion in Lee's Army.*[3] Other works followed on Jefferson Davis and Jackson. Then came a much better book on Lee, *Life and Letters of Robert Edward Lee, Soldier and Man* (New York, 1908).

Not only was Jones writing on Lee and the Army of Northern Virginia. He had another very important task. In the autumn of 1869, forty-four men met in New Orleans. They sought to "create an organization which might effect the collection and preservation of such papers and records as might be available in preserving a true history of the causes and events of the Civil War." The result was the Southern Historical Society. Benjamin M. Palmer, a Presbyterian clergyman, was elected as the first president. Robert E. Lee was named one of the vice-presidents.

Four years of struggle followed. The treasury had a grand total of $177. The future looked dark. Then in 1873 another meeting was held at White Sulphur Springs. The headquarters was transferred to Richmond. Jubal A. Early, the ranking Confederate officer in Virginia, was named president. The goal of the group was expanded to include "the collection, classification, preservation, and final publication in some form to be hereafter determined, of all the documents and facts bearing upon the eventful history of the past four years."

In 1874 Jones stepped into the picture. He became the secretary-treasurer of the society. He was well suited for the job, having been a chaplain in both the Second and Third Corps.

J. William Jones, the cleric, was the "leader behind the establishment and organization of the Southern Historical Society Papers (SHSP). He solicited all the early material." He wrote a major article on refuting mistreatment of Northern prisoners. And in 1876 "publication of the SHSP began on a bimonthly basis." Jones did most of the work in the first fourteen years. When he retired, he suggested methods of continued finance.

Jones had started his work at the University of Virginia. In 1893 he returned for a brief while, this time as chaplain. Retirement was nearing. This gave him more time to devote to history and writing. His days and hours were full of efforts for the Confederate Memorial Association, and the United Confederate Veterans. He was chaplain-general of the UCV. Jones was also a trustee for the erection fund of Battle Abbey in Richmond.

General Douglas MacArthur constantly referred to "Duty, Honor, Country," and "the Corps, the Corps, the Corps." With John William Jones it was the South, History, and the Confederacy, and the rich heritage of that period.

The preacher Jackson knew died in March 1909, at the home of a son in Columbus, Georgia. Funeral services for the literary giant and historian were held on Sunday, March 21, 1909, in Richmond.

For anyone interested in religion in the Army of Northern Virginia, Jones's book, *Christ in Camp*, is a must. Jones was a part of the movement he writes about. He took a different approach to the Confederate defeat than many others. He accepted reality and worked to bind up the wounds of the war. At the same time, he felt that the revivals were good, and produced a wholesome, lasting effect.[4]

 Jones and the *preachers Jackson knew* were evangelicals. They stressed eternal life, salvation through the new birth, the worth of the human soul, the wages of sin, and the Crucifixion and Resurrection.[5]

The lads from the South were exposed to many temptations and situations in the military. They were away from home, neighbors, and the church. They became aware of how quickly life could end. They answered the calls of the preachers who stressed, "Prepare to meet thy God."

Many of them carried well-worn Bibles on the march. There were prayer meetings around many a campfire, and those on guard duty late at night used the time to pray and meditate. Many of them resigned or committed their life to Christ in the same manner as Jackson. Jones again was a part of these moments.[6]

Jones was convinced "that Jesus was in our camps with wonderful power, and that no army in all history – had in it as much real, evangelical religion and devout piety as the Army of Northern Virginia."[7]

Jones shared the story of the Liberty Hall Volunteers, a company of seventy-two men from Washington College in Lexington. All the officers were Christians, including the captain, a son of Dr. White, Jackson's pastor. Half of the company belonged to evangelical churches, and one-fourth of them were ministerial candidates. This company is a story in itself, and is the subject of a book by Dr. W. G. Bean.[8]

The story of the involvement of ministers is another saga. Dr. Junkin and White helped to mould the Christian life of Jackson. Dr. Graham, although born in the North, was a Confederate at heart. Lacy and Hopkins were chaplains, and Dr. Hoge was a member of the Home Guard in Richmond.

Jackson's concern for the spiritual welfare of his men was amazing. After First Manassas, men of the Seventeenth Virginia built a chapel. So did the Thirteenth Virginia. Jones recalled preaching in the chapel of the Stonewall brigade to an overflow crowd. One of the men serving as chief usher that autumn Sunday was none other than Thomas J. Jackson.[9]

Jones tells of camping in the lovely Shenandoah Valley in the early days of the war. Camp was pitched under the canopy of heaven and the stars above. The men gathered water and made their campfires.

> Before the bivouac is quiet for the night there assembles a little group at some convenient spot, . . . who strike up some dear old hymn which recalls hallowed memories of home and loved ones, and of the dear old church far away. . . . From all parts of the bivouac men hasten to the spot; the song grows clearer and louder, and in a few moments a very large congregation has assembled. And as the chaplain reads some appropriate Scripture, leads in fervent prayer, and speaks words of earnest counsel, faithful and admonition or solemn warning,
>
> > "Something on the soldier's cheek
> > Washes off the stain of powder."[10]

Jones felt that short sermons on the march often were the most effective. The Reverend Mr. Taylor was preaching at 7:30 on the morning of the Battle of Cross Keys. The preacher made one last plea for the men to prepare to meet their Maker.

Before Second Manassas, Union shells started to fall in the midst of Confederates assembled for worship. Colonel Walker gave the order to move back. This was done during the singing of a hymn. Jones then continued the service by preaching on "Except ye repent ye shall all likewise perish." Later, Jones found that at least twenty shells had fallen where the men had originally gathered.

Jones also had fond memories of an experience near Hagerstown. On the banks of the Antietam Creek, on the way to Gettysburg, the soldiers sang as "one of the chaplains led down into the historic stream fourteen veterans who a few months before had fought at Sharpsburg, and were now enlisting under the banner of the Cross. This was June 28, 1863.

One of Jones's fond memories of Jackson occurred near Hamilton's Crossing in the spring of 1863. Jones was on his way to a meeting of the chaplains when Jackson overtook him. The general was riding alone. After inquiring where the chaplain was going, he dismounted and walked several miles with Jones. His main interest was in the spiritual welfare of the troops and "how best to promote them."

In a note to the Presbyterian General Assembly he said, "Our chaplains, . . . encamped in the same neighborhood, should have their meetings, and through God's blessing devise successful plans for spiritual conquests.[11]

Jones was grateful for the commitment of Robert E. Lee. The commanding general thought a lot like Jackson. As early as 1862, he issued an order stating that "all duties except those of inspection will be suspended during Sunday, to afford the troops rest and to enable them to attend religious services."[12]

Jones had his first interview with Lee in February of 1864. At that time, he and Beverly Lacy went to see Lee in behalf of the Chaplains' Committee. The purpose was to urge better use of the Sabbath in the camps along the Rapidan. His eyes brightened when told of the revival that was sweeping the camps. "In his simple, feeling words, he expressed his delight, we forgot the great warrior, and only remembered that we were communing with an humble, earnest Christian."

Lee issued General Order 15, dated February 15, 1864. He called attention to the fact that the army had already been reminded of a proper observance of the Sabbath. Now he was repeating the orders. He stated that he had learned with great pleasure "that in many brigades convenient houses of worship have been erected."

Once again, he directed that none but strictly essential duties were to be performed on the Sabbath. Tasks were to be done only if necessary for "the safety, health, or comfort," of the men and animals. Inspections were to be held at a time other than at a worship hour. Inspections were not to interfere "with the attendance of the men on divine service at the customary hour in the morning."

Officers were to insure the maintenance of order and quiet near the place of worship, and "prohibit anything that may tend to disturb or interrupt religious exercises." Jackson would have concurred with this.

J. William Jones first met Thomas J. Jackson on July 4, 1861. Confederate forces were drawn up in line of battle at Darkesville, opposing the advance of General Patterson and Union troops.

A friend of Jones's, C. F. Fry, wanted permission to distribute Bibles and Christian tracts within the camp. Jackson being in command, Jones went to see him. Jones described what took place:

> I have a vivid recollection of how he impressed me. Dressed in a simple Virginia uniform, apparently about thirty-seven years old, six feet high, medium size, grey eyes that seemed to look through you, light brown hair. and a countenance in which deep benevolence seemed mingled with uncompromising sternness, he seemed to me to have about him nothing at all of the "pomp and circumstance of war," but every element which enters into the skilful leader, and the indomitable, energetic soldier who was always ready for the fight.

Replying to the request, Jackson said, "Certainly, sir; it will give me great pleasure to grant all such permits." Jackson stated that the Bible salesman was more than welcome, "It will give me great pleasure to help you in your work in every way in my power. I am more anxious than I can express that my men should be not only good soldiers of their country, but also good soldiers of the Cross."

There in the fields north of Winchester, Jones says, "I felt that I had met a man of deep-toned piety, who carried his religion into every affair of life, and who was destined to make his mark in the war."[13]

We have already said that Jackson's military career is history. Many have written about his relationship with the generals and the troops. But Jones and the other clergymen saw a lot of the general. He shared with them his deep feelings, and discussed theology instead of strategy. From his own contact with Jackson, and the experiences others shared with him, Jones felt that the general's Christian character was "well worthy of earnest study."

His self-discipline and high regard for being on time is seen in church matters as well as the military. While a deacon of the Lexington Church, he went to a meeting where important business was to be transacted. Normally he started at the appointed time. This night, however, one member was absent.

Pacing back and forth with his watch in his hand, he asked to be excused. Off he went to the home of the absentee member. Ringing the doorbell very strongly, the other deacon responded. Jackson let him have it. "Mr. – – –, it is eight minutes after 8 o'clock." "Yes, major," replied the dumbfounded deacon. "I am aware of that, but I did not have time to go out tonight."

That was the wrong thing to say. Just as he was never prone to accept the excuses of his military lieutenants, Jackson was not about to accept the excuse of the Presbyterian deacon.

"Didn't have time?" retorted Jackson. "Why, sir, I should not suppose that you had time for anything else. Did we not set apart this hour for the service of the church? How then can you put aside your obligations in the matter?" Turning on his heel, Jackson started back to the meeting. The rebuked elder soon followed.

Jackson's work with black children in Lexington is described in the chapter on Dr. White. He had another ministry with the blacks in the area. Prior to the war he was a collector for the Rockbridge Bible Society. When it came time to make a report, he surprised everyone by saying he had several contributions from the blacks. He said, "They are poor, but ought not on that account to be denied the sweet privilege of helping so good a cause." He also reported contributions from everyone in his district with the exception of one lady. The next day he saw her, and she gave to the society.

Dr. William Brown, editor of the *Central Presbyterian,* visited the troops around Centreville during the summer of 1861. A friend told him that Jackson was crazy. Brown asked, "Why do you say that?"

> Why I frequently meet him out in the woods walking back and forth muttering to himself incoherent sentences and gesticulating wildly, and at such times he seems utterly oblivious of my presence and of everything else.[14]

The next night Brown bunked with Jackson, and the two had a long talk. The conversation turned to prayer and to Jackson's favorite theme, "the means of promoting personal holiness in camp." Sharing with Brown, Jackson stated,

> I find that it greatly helps me in fixing my mind and quickening my devotions to give articulate utterance to my prayers, and hence I am

11

in the habit of going off into the woods, where I can be alone and speak audibly to myself the prayers I would pour out to God. I was first annoyed that I was compelled to keep my eyes open to avoid running against the trees and stumps; but upon investigating the matter I do not find that the Scriptures require us to close our eyes in prayer, and the exercise has proven to me very delightful and profitable.[15]

This conversation assured Brown that Jackson was not crazy, but a man of the Book, and a man of deep piety.

He believed in praying without ceasing. There was grace at meals, and whenever "I take a draught of water I always pause, . . . to lift up my heart to God in thanks and prayer for the water of life. Whenever I drop a letter into the box at the postoffice I send a petition along with it for God's blessing upon the person to whom it is sent. When I break the seal of a letter just received I stop to pray to God that He may prepare me for its contents and make it a messenger of good. When I go to my classroom and await the arrangement of the cadets in their places, that is my time to intercede with God for them. And so of every other familiar act of the day.

After Manassas, Tom wrote to Dr. White in Lexington. The folks were sure it was a message describing the battle. However, it was a note and money for the work among the blacks. (See the chapter on Dr. White.)
He also wrote to Anna:

My preservation was entirely due, as was the glorious victory, to our God, to whom be all honor, praise, and glory. . . . Whilst great credit is due to other parts of our gallant army, God made my brigade more instrumental than any other in repulsing the main attack. This is for your information only – say nothing about it. Let others speak praise, not myself.[16]

On August 5, he wrote, "My darling, never distrust our God, who doeth all things well. In due time He will manifest all His pleasure which is all His people should desire."

Jackson loved the Shenandoah Valley. Later in the year, he learned that Lee had gone to the western part of the state. In a letter to his wife, he expressed, "I would like to go there and give my feeble aid, as an instrument in the hand of Providence in retrieving . . . that part of my native State."

Then in late October Dr. White came to visit the camp near Centreville. During this visit, Jackson ministered to his pastor, more than the clergyman ministered to him. (Once again, see the chapter on Dr. White.)

Just after his arrival in Winchester, Jackson went to the Kent Street Presbyterian Church, and soon became good friends with James and Fanny Graham. And on January 1, 1862, he asked the preacher and his wife to care for Anna until his return from the Romney expedition. When he returned late in January, he also moved into the manse. He and Graham shared in theological discussions, and the Jacksons took part in family devotion with the minister's family. In fact, the general and the preacher took turns leading the Bible readings and prayers. And just prior to leaving Winchester in March of 1862, Jackson, dressed for combat, had a very moving prayer with his adopted family. But more about all of this in the chapter on the Grahams.

April 13 finds Jackson headquartered at the Reverend Mr. Rude's just north of New Market. Here he also shared in devotions, and on the thirteenth, distributed religious tracts in the camp of General Taliaferro. The general also sent aides to other camps on the same mission.

On May 20, Jackson met Richard Taylor and his Louisiana troops near New Market. Tom was very much impressed with the military appearance of these troops. He then spent the night at Taylor's camp. Richard writes, "If silence be golden, he was a "bonanza.' . . . Praying and fighting appeared to be his idea of the 'whole duty of man.' "

The next day Jackson and Taylor rode together across the Massanutten Mountains into the Luray Valley, headed for Front Royal. "I began to think that Jackson was an unconscious poet, and . . . an ardent lover of nature. Once again, Jackson said very little. Taylor thought he was riding and praying.

"This Is My Father's World" may have been one of Tom's favorite hymns. If not, it certainly expresses part of his faith. He loved to pray in the woods, he rode and prayed, and one of his rituals in Lexington was to get up early, take a walk at daybreak and listen to the chirping of the birds.

James Power Smith also attests to Jackson's interest in everything.

> Not only was he sensitive to every touch of human sorrow, but no man was ever more susceptible to impressions from the physical world. The hum of bees, the fragrance of clover fields, the tender streaks of dawn, the dewy brightness of early spring, the mellow glories of matured autumn, all by turns charmed and tranquillized him.

The eye that glowed in battle, grew soft in contemplating the beauty of a flower. The ear that thrilled with the thunder of the cannonade, drank in with innocent delight the song of birds and the prattle of children's voices.

Jackson hated profanity. In the advance on Winchester, some of the troops took cover. Richard Taylor cussed them out and urged them on.[17]

Tom, who was riding nearby, heard the profanity. "He placed his hand on my shoulder, and said in a gentle voice, 'I am afraid you are a wicked fellow.' " With that he turned and rode back to the pike.

Several weeks later, Hunter McGuire was to be rebuked. The Winchester physician was removing wounded troops from a church in Port Republic. He was urging the men and horses along with choice words. Jackson took him to task.[18]

McGuire also got in trouble making a remark about John Harman. The former stagecoach operator from Staunton was very efficient. However, he was extremely profane. On one occasion he was ill. A few days later, Jackson asked about Harman's condition. In reply, McGuire said, "He must be better. He's swearing like a trooper again." When Jackson saw Harman, he rebuked him for the profanity. Harman had a short temper and was out to get McGuire for telling on him. Needless to say, McGuire stayed out of Harman's sight until the temperamental officer cooled down.

Throughout the Valley Campaign as he divided and conquered the commands sent against him, Jackson followed one of his main principles, "Trust in God, and do not take counsel of your fears."

After the glorious victory at Winchester, Jackson thanked his command, and ordered a day of thanksgiving. While most of the wording may be that of R. L. Dabney, the thought and content are consistent with Jackson's approach. The General Order published on May 26, 1862, stated:

> The General Commanding would warmly express to the officers and men under his command his joy in their achievements and his thanks for their brilliant gallantry in action. . . .But his chief duty today, and that of the army, is to recognize devoutly the hand of Providence in the brilliant successes of the past three days which have given us the results of a great victory without great losses. . . . For this purpose the troops will remain in camp today, suspending, as far as practicable, all military exercises, and the chaplains of regiments will hold Divine service in their several charges at 4 o'clock today.

On Sunday night, Jackson went to see his Winchester friends, the Reverend Mr. and Mrs. Graham.

About a month later, Jackson was en route to join Lee before Richmond. On the twenty-second he was at Fredericks Hall. He spent the day at services, and in private devotions. The next morning, he was up at 1:00 a.m. and rode until midafternoon to meet Lee, and then started back again in early evening. This was a ride of over one hundred miles in a little over twenty-four hours.

On the thirteenth of July 1862, Jackson rode into Richmond. Supposedly this was his first visit to the capital of the Confederacy since his rise to fame. His purpose, among other things, was to go to church. His destination was Second Presbyterian Church, where the pastor was Moses Drury Hoge, the subject of another chapter.

The rest of July and early August was spent in the Gordonsville area. Jackson sought quarters with another clergyman, the Reverend Mr. Ewing. Once again he entered into theological discussions, and shared in family devotions.

The Second Virginia Infantry, from what is now the West Virginia Eastern panhandle, and the northern section of the Shenandoah Valley, gave to Jackson Henry Kyd

Douglas, Hunter Holmes McGuire, and J. Wells Hawks. Douglas was from Shepherdstown, McGuire from Winchester, and Hawks from Charles Town. They were all first rate staff officers. From the ranks of the Second Virginia came Rev. A. C. Hopkins, a native of Martinsburg, and pastor of the Presbyterian Church in Charles Town.

Hopkins relates the story of a prayer meeting during the Second Manassas Campaign. Colonel Baylor and Captain White were both in attendance. They prayed together that night, and both fell in action the next day. Jackson was deeply touched by their deaths. We'll pick up this story in the chapter on Dr. White.

After the battle, Hunter McGuire, Jackson's surgeon, talked with the commander. The Winchester physician said, "General, this day has been won by nothing but stark and stern fighting." "No," replied Jackson, "it has been won by nothing but the blessing and protection of Providence." Then the general looked up at the stars overlooking the battlefield.

Jackson closed his report on Second Manassas by saying, "For these great and signal victories our sincere and humble thanks are due to Almighty God. We should in all things acknowledge the hand of Him who reigns in heaven and rules among the armies of the world. . . . We can but express the grateful conviction that God was with us, and gave us the victory; and unto His holy name be all the praise."

Throughout his career, Jackson made frequent mentions of Divine Providence in his letters to Anna, and in his official reports and communiques. On August 31, he wrote to his wife:

> We were engaged with the enemy at and near Manassas Junction Tuesday and Wednesday, and again near the battle-field of Manassas on Thursday, Friday, and Saturday; in all of which God gave us the victory. May he ever be with us, and we ever be his devoted people, is my earnest prayer. It greatly encourages me to feel that so many of God's people are praying for that part of our force under my command. The Lord has answered their prayers. . . . And I pray that He will make our arms entirely successful, and that all glory will be given to His holy name, and none of it to man. God has blessed and preserved me through His great mercy. . . .

In early September, the Lexington Presbytery passed a special resolution about Jackson and his troops. More about that in the pages about Dr. White.

By Sunday, September 7, the Army of Northern Virginia was across the Potomac, and Jackson was camped south of Frederick. Young James P. Smith, soon to come on staff, went into town to visit the church of his boyhood.

There were no evening services at the Presbyterian Church, so Jackson went to the German Reformed Church. Henry Douglas and Jackson describe the evening.[19] Jackson soon fell asleep which he lamented in a letter to his wife. The preacher, Rev. Daniel Zacharias, was praised for praying for Mr. Lincoln in the presence of Jackson. Douglas states that Jackson did not hear the prayer, and had he been asked permission would no doubt have said, "Go right ahead and pray for Mr. Lincoln, he needs it." Frederick impressed Jackson, reminding him of Lexington and home, and causing him to feel a twinge of homesickness.

Riding with the Reverend Mr. Hopkins on the way to disrupt railroad traffic at Martinsburg, and to capture Harpers Ferry, Jackson and the Reverend Mr. Hopkins discussed the prayer meeting the night before Colonel Baylor and Captain White, his pastor's son, were killed.

The Second Virginia was at the head of the column. Hopkins related that Baylor had made a profession of faith. The general replied, "I am glad of it; I hope he died a Christian; he needed only Christianity to make him a model man. . . ."[20]

October 1862 brought rest and regrouping at Bunker Hill and also revival. Dr. Stiles, whom we shall meet later, seems to have been the leader.

Henry Kyd Douglas describes the services at Bunker Hill:

> Meetings were held in one of the camps nearly every night. Jackson often attended these meetings and took part in their exercises, offering a fervent prayer . . . to God in the midst of the camps. One night will illustrate.
>
> He asked me to walk across the fields to the camp of the Stonewall Brigade to a prayer meeting, and we went striding over the rough soil. General Jackson's step at any time could hardly be called a walk;

17

with his heavy army boots on he simply plodded along, talking as we went about sundry things. . . . As we approached camp – it was after night – he was recognized. A runner sprinted on before and gave the news. I noticed as we approached the tents, in many of them were sitting squads of fours, around a candle in an inverted bayonet. stuck in the ground as a candlestick, absorbed in games of cards. As the General approached, the light would go out, the cards would be put down in place, just as they were held, the players would crawl out and fall in behind; and when he had reached the place of prayer, lo, the camp was there. Bowed heads, bent knees, hats off, silence. Stonewall Jackson was kneeling to the Lord of Hosts, in prayer for his people! Not as sound disturbed his voice as it ascended to Heaven in their behalf and, in their faith, the stars seemed to move softly and make no noise. When he left, a line of soldiers followed him in escort to the edge of the camp. . . . From a scene like this one, made vivid by the pencil of Vizetelly, came, I fancy, the engraving, "Prayer in Stonewall Jackson's Camp."[21]

This was the autumn of 1862 at Bunker Hill. What a time it must have been. Jackson at prayer, evangelistic sermons, old-time Gospel singing, and soldiers making decisions for Jesus Christ.

In November, General Jackson took a rare day off to dine with Hunter McGuire's folks in Winchester, and to have his picture taken. The Reverend Mr. Graham will tell us about that later.

While the army was camped near Winchester, A. C. Hopkins of the Second Virginia "received a message from General Jackson, . . . requesting me to prepare and send him a list of chaplains, their regiments, etc., in his old division." Jackson, who felt he should be a spiritual leader as well as their general, also wanted to know what regiments were without chaplains, and what their denominational preference might be if chaplains could be secured.

Before the month was over, he was to pray for the last time with the Grahams, and then in Fredericksburg. James P. Smith will relate that story later. And Jackson was to ride to see the wounded General Gregg, making sure that everything was alright between the two of them, and making sure of the condition of the officer's soul as he prepared to step out into eternity.

Jackson witnessed in many ways. A correspondent saw

Jackson on the field of battle, and the incident made more of an impact on him than anything he had ever read on religion. "While the battle was raging and the bullets were flying, Jackson rode by, calm as if he were at home, but his head was raised toward heaven, and his lips were moving, evidently in prayer.

Staff officers often entered his tent late at night and found him kneeling in prayer. These were not short moments. Sometimes, Jackson spent an hour or more in prayer.

Jones also shares that after a victory is won, "The army is drawn up in line, the general dismounts from his horse, and then, in the presence of his . . . troops, with head uncovered, and bent awe-stricken to the ground, the voice of the good man, . . . is now heard subdued and calm, as if overcome by the presence of the Supreme Being. . . ."

Jones and Smith tell the story of seeing an officer wrapped in his overcoat. The marks of his rank could not be seen. He was in the rear of a battery reading his Bible. A chaplain talked of the impending battle. But the Bible reader turned the conversation to the Scriptures. The chaplain was surprised to find it none other than General Jackson.

During the stay in winter quarters at Moss Neck, Jackson often entered into theological discussions with his staff, and read religious books from the Corbin library. Preachers came and went from his office. During the winter, he made an appeal for chaplains, and brought Beverly Tucker Lacy to headquarters to coordinate work among the chaplains. We shall read later about the weekly meetings and about the daily devotions Lacy conducted at headquarters.

During the winter of 1863, the Stonewall brigade built a chapel and revival broke out in Fredericksburg. One of the biggest moments in Jackson's life came in April of 1863 when Tucker Lacy baptized little Julia Jackson at Yerby's.

And during his last days at Chandler's, Jackson talked with James Power Smith about deep spiritual concerns. The general stated he believed the Bible had rules for

19

everything. With a smile on his face he asked James, "Can you tell me where the Bible gives generals a model for their official reports of battles?" Smith replied that he had never thought of looking in the Bible for such things. Jackson had an answer. There were excellent examples, particularly in the narrative of Joshua and his battle with the Amalekites. That account had clarity, brevity, fairness, and modesty, and said Jackson, "It traces the victory to its right source, the blessing of God."[22]

This chapter is meant to be an overview of the spiritual life of Jackson. Where the ministers are involved, we touch lightly upon the event, and then go into detail in the chapter involving Jackson and the preacher concerned. When military figures share the account, we go into more detail.

Jones had profound respect for Lacy and Jackson. He says, "Dr. Lacy was a genial gentleman, an indefatigable worker, and a powerful and effective preacher."[23]

Jones called at Jackson's headquarters in the spring of 1863. The general was just going into a prayer meeting, presumably the 10:00 a.m. session. John accepted the invitation to attend. "I shall never forget the power, comprehensiveness, and tender pathos of the prayer he made. . . ."

Just before Chancellorsville, Jones dined with Jackson at the mess hall of Second Corps Headquarters. The general did not want to talk of military matters, but of spiritual matters. He discussed personal piety, and obstacles to spiritual growth in the military. He also talked of how to get more good chaplains for the army.

On another occasion, when A. P. Hill and R. S. Ewell were waiting for orders from headquarters, Hill remarked, "Well, I guess Jackson wants time to pray about it." Ewell went to Tom's tent, and sure enough, Jackson was in prayer. And Richard was deeply impressed. He said, "If that's religion, I must have it."[24]

On another occasion Lacy and others visited General Lee. As they prepared to leave, Bev Lacy told the general that many in the army were praying for him. Lee's face flushed, tears came into his eyes, and with a voice choking with emotion, said, "Please thank them for that, sir—I warmly appreciate it. And I can only say that I am nothing but a poor sinner trusting in Christ alone for salvation, and need all the prayers they can offer for me." This statement reflects Jackson's faith, Christian walk, and humility.

Jones served the Baptist Church in Lexington for six years. He always found the blacks to speak very highly of the man they called Stonewall. They were grateful for his concern and work among them. In fact, "the first contribution toward the erection of the beautiful bronze statue, which now decks the hero's grave, was from the negro Baptist Church in Lexington."[25] The pastor and many members of the congregation had attended Jackson's Sunday School in days gone by.

Jones felt two verses summarized Jackson's life. "Lord, what wilt Thou have me to do?" and the words describing Saint Paul, "Not slothful in business, fervent in prayer, serving the Lord."

At Moss Neck, Jackson walked through the woods with Jones one day, and encouraged him to write to leading preachers in different denominations, urging them to come and serve the troops, if only for a short period of time.

Jackson said, "Tell them for me that they must come, and that they will never find a grander field of usefulnes than right here among these noble men, these patriot heroes of our Southland."[26]

The general then talked about another favorite subject, "growing in grace," Jones wanted to sit at Jackson's feet and learn all he could.

As the war went on Jones had fond memories of seeing Lee and Stuart at church, but his favorite memory was the gleam in Jackson's eye as he ushered men into the services to hear the Gospel. And a prayer meeting that Jackson led just before his death would linger in Jones's mind until "I meet him on that brighter shore."

II

DR. GEORGE JUNKIN

"Of my family I know but little," said George Junkin. They came from Scotland. George II was on the throne of England when Joseph Junkin and Elizabeth Wallace crossed the Susquehanna River at Harris's Ferry, now Harrisburg, and moved into the lovely Cumberland Valley. Joseph and Elizabeth "took up" five hundred acres of land, "including the present site of Kingston," Pennsylvania. This is north of Carlisle on which is now U.S. 11.

In a stone house in the Kingston area, another Joseph was born. This was the father of George. "I remember this house distinctly. It stood over a spring, directly north of the stone tavern, which now (1861) stands one-third of a mile east of Kingston."[1]

George's father fought in the Revolutionary War, commanding a company of Cumberland County Volunteers at the Battle of Brandywine, narrowly escaping with his life.

George's mother, Eleanor Cochran, was born near Waynesboro, Pennsylvania. As a girl, she was nearly captured by the Indians. The schoolmaster was killed, and the biggest male student tomahawked in the head. All the pupils were taken prisoner with the exception of one. Eleanor missed it all because providentially she was kept home because of "flax pulling."

Joseph Junkin and Eleanor Cochran were married on May 24, 1779. They had fourteen children. George, the sixth child and fourth son, was born in the lovely stone house on November 1, 1790.[2]

Looking back over his life, George writes:

> Nothing occurs to my memory worthy of note until 1804. That year, for the first, I made 'a hand' at the sickle in my father's harvesting. The sickle, in those days, was the chief instrument for cutting grain. The fields were laid out in 'lands' of eight feet wide, and two hands took 'a land,' and must always clean up the right hand furrow. . . .

It seems as though George's partner took advantage of his youth, and lack of knowledge about the job and made him do twice the amount of work. We mention this job because Tom Jackson in all probability did the same work as a boy in the hills of West Virginia.

The summer and fall of 1804 brought sickness, fever, and ague to the Cumberland Valley. The entire Junkin family was stricken. Twelve of them were ill at one time.

The illness, plus the removal of the Indian problem, led Mr. Junkin to head west. In April of 1806, the Junkin family moved near Mercer, to a land of great beauty and fertile soil. It took a week for the family to make the journey. They trekked through deep forests, and over steep hills. There were streams and rivers to ford and at times, they had to be ferried across. Part of their belongings had to be left in Pittsburg as they discarded all but the essential items.

George spent three years helping to establish the farm. He made a nice cherry cradle for his brother, and one summer killed seventeen rattlesnakes. The new home was called "Hope Mills."

In May of 1807 the Junkin family went via carriage to Pittsburg for a shopping trip. George went along to enter "the grammar school of Jefferson College" in Canonsburg, Pennsylvania.

Young George soon developed a talent for self-expression and became very good in the literary field. He became a member of the Franklin Literary Society. He won top honors and was regarded as an excellent student.

From early boyhood, George seems to have been a very sensitive soul. At the age of ten he started to think seriously about Christianity and the salvation of his soul. He later wrote, "I felt the burden of sin, but was long in obtain-

23

ing a clear view of the method of deliverance." Although regular and faithful at worship and other church meetings, something seemed to be missing.

Then in 1811 he heard the Reverend James Galloway preach a sermon. And, says George, "I found it. The way of deliverance from sin by the blood of Christ – of justification by His righteousness, – of santification by His Spirit, all became plain. My doubts and fears passed away, and I came to enjoy a good hope. I found more comfort in secret devotion. I used to walk out in the morning for secret prayer and devotion."[3]

George united with the church, took Holy Communion, and he enjoyed "a general calm and steady hope ever since." While home on vacation, he shared a room with Mr. Galloway. The two of them had deep theological discussions. On March 12, 1812, the clergyman married George's sister Agnes.

The spring brought joy. But just as autumn brings falling leaves and frost, the fall of 1812 brought sadness to the Junkins. George's mother fell and broke her back. When George heard the news he rode thirty-six miles, and had to turn back because of a swollen stream. Detouring, the trip amounted to sixty-five miles, "the longest horseback ride I ever made in one day."[4]

His mother told him that she must die. She spoke calmly and triumphantly of her passage. Mother Junkin told George, "The Lord will take care of all of you if you only trust in Him." She then turned and looked lovingly at each member of the family, gazing last upon her husband. Then she breathed her last and went to a greater home with her Lord.

In October of 1813, George left for New York City to study theology with Dr. Mason. For part of the way, George traveled with his brother John, "the only one of seven brothers who was not either a minister or an elder in the church." John was a very devout man, an army officer, and destined to die young. When the two parted, it was their final meeting.

Although the careers of the *preachers Jackson knew* are

most interesting, it is not our intention to go into detail. Their memoirs tell about those days. Our purpose is to relate the story of the men and Jackson.

Junkin studied with Dr. Mason in New York, and then filled several appointments, considered missionary in nature. His first service was on September 16, 1816, at Butler, Pennsylvania. Often he preached in homes in the woods of western Pennsylvania.

On June 29, 1818, he was ordained as an evangelist at the Associate Reformed Church in Gettysburg. Forty-five years later, he would be back in the same church, caring for those who had fallen in battle.

Meanwhile, he had met and fallen in love with the daughter of Rev. Ebenezer Dickey of Chester County. After much thought though, he decided she was not the right one.

His next assignment was Milton, Pennsylvania, and on June 1, 1819, he was married to Miss Julia Rush Miller. They spent the better part of eleven years at Milton. He was a good preacher, and spoke out strongly against the evils of alcohol. And he published *The Religious Farmer*. The title describes the contents.

In 1832, Junkin accepted the presidency of Lafayette College in Easton, Pennsylvania. "A farm of some seventy acres, with spacious mansion and other buildings, was leased for the temporary accommodation of the institution. The farm lay on the south bank of the Lehigh, adjoining Easton. . . ." He had his work cut out for him, but with prayer and hard work achieved great success.

Junkin's biographer says,

> His intellectual power, great experience and skill as a Presbyter, and his devout and earnest zeal for everything that promised to promote the good of the church and the glory of her Head, were soon recognized by his brethren. . . . Both pastors and the people of the congregations sought and welcomed his labors; and, although he was so devoted to the great work of education, he loved to preach the gospel. . . . He often preached for the pastors of Easton and of the surrounding country. . . .

These experiences occurred during his presidency of Lafayette College. Rarely was there a Sunday that he did not preach once, usually it was two or three times. The word zeal characterized his life. It was a trait that T. J. Jackson saw in Junkin, and although the two did not always agree, there was a profound mutual respect. Jackson, as he did with most preachers who were dedicated and zealous, stood in awe at times of Junkin.

In 1833 Jefferson College conferred upon Junkin the honorary degree of Doctor of Divinity. In those days, such an honor was rare, and meant more then than today.

At Lafayette, Junkin was like a father and pastor to his students. He visited in the dorms, conversed with them about their problems and spiritual needs, and prayed with them. When illness struck or problems at home, he was there with the students.

> This deep affection for his pupils was one of the secrets of Dr. J's great power in governing young men in college. . . . His pupils found out that Dr. Junkin had heart as well as head.

His compassion and ministry to his students was made even deeper when on March 15, 1834, a little son died, and Dr. Junkin walked through the Valley of the Shadow.

In the summer of 1848 the Trustees of Washington College in Lexington, Virginia, elected Dr. Junkin as their president. His work at Lafayette and Miami was well known. He was highly respected in Presbyterian circles, and Washington College had been founded by a minister in that denomination, Rev. William Graham. Originally called "Liberty Hall," it now went by the name of the father of our country. Mr. Washington had refused funds from the state of Virginia when the state tried to express its affection after the Revolutionary War. As a compromise, he directed that a gift of stock in the James River Canal be used for an institution of higher learning.

Dr. Junkin made the trip to Lexington to meet with the officials and look over the town and the campus. He must have fallen in love with the area as most people do. When he came back, he was convinced that "the hand of God was again beckoning him away from his 'lovely Lafayette.' " The Trustees of Washington College were basically Presbyterians, and they shared Junkin's views of doctrine and morality.

Some of his friends felt that inasmuch as he had endured the labors of starting a school, he deserved the opportunity to go to one already well established. He also needed a milder climate, for the sake of his son Joseph who had difficulty breathing.

Junkin had spent thirteen years at Lafayette, and three and a half at Miami. Folks were amazed at the progress of Lafayette. They were also struck by the distinguished list of graduates.

Much of the gratitude felt by the trustees, community, and student body was expressed at the 1848 graduation ceremonies. At the close of the ceremonies, members of the senior class approached Junkin to bid him farewell. Tears rolled down many cheeks, and people were too filled to speak. One hundred and twenty students came forward to take the hand, not just of the college president, but the hand of their friend. "The young men wept, the President wept, the audience was in tears, whilst no sound was heard except the quiet tread of those noble young men as they advanced to the dias, pressed the President's hand, and retired." One witness, deeply moved by the proceedings, said, "This is the proudest day in George Junkin's history." He was indeed, "The Father and Founder" of Lafayette College.[5] Later twenty-six young men from Lafayette transferred to Washington College to continue their education under Junkin.

Washington College was to be a challenge for Junkin. There were many rivals for students in the Shenandoah Valley. The University of Virginia claimed many, and others went to nearby Hampden-Sydney, or the Virginia Military Institute in Lexington. Junkin commenced his duties in the Shenandoah Valley in October of 1848, but was not formally inaugurated until June of 1849.

He was soon caught up in the mood and discussion of the day. In Pennsylvania he had resisted abolition on the grounds that it was trying to break up the peace of the country, and divide the Union. He feared that the movement would lead to war and bloodshed. Yet he never believed in

27

slavery, and felt it was morally wrong. Now in Virginia, he was in an area where people had strong feelings both pro and con.[6]

Junkin had quite a trip to Lexington. Now travel from Easton to Lexington can be made in six hours or less by car, but in 1848, the family took a steamboat from Baltimore to Fredericksburg, changed to a train which took them to Gordonsville, and the last miles were covered by stagecoach.

The faculty consisted of four professors. The most prominent name was that of Major Daniel Harvey Hill.

Sadly, Lexington did not help the breathing problems of Joseph. Brother John, who was a doctor, took him to sunny Florida. However, on April 3, 1849, Joseph died. Apparently it was tuberculosis.

Otherwise, life in Lexington was rather routine. There were the usual administrative duties, and the planning for the growth of the college. Junkin also preached whenever he had the opportunity. He soon established a service for the students in the chapel, and for a time supplied a small church nearby.

> The society of Lexington was very congenial to his tastes and to those of his family. It was a highly intelligent community. . . . The Presbyterian Church was the largest and most influential in the place, and the prominent men of the community threw the weight of their influence in favor of religion and good morals. . . . The excellent minister Rev. William S. White, D.D., was pastor of the Presbyterian church . . . during most of the time of Dr. Junkin's sojourn in that place, and with him he had much pleasant fraternal intercourse.

For the most part, the years were good in Lexington, with the exception of personal sadness, and the slavery issue.

When the Reverend Mr. Junkin moved to Lexington, he was the proud father of nine children. The two most prominent were his daughters, Ellie and Margaret. Ellie was to link Junkin with the life of Thomas J. Jackson, and Margaret with Major Preston, also of the Virginia Military Institute faculty.

As we have already seen, a son died in infancy, and Joseph in the spring of 1849. John was a doctor and had located in Trenton, New Jersey. He took a leave to go to

Florida to be with Joseph during his last days. George, named after his father, had just completed his college work, and had begun the practice of law in Philadelphia. A fourth son, Ebenezer Dickey, had graduated from Lafayette, and was teaching in Fredericksburg. William Finney taught for a while in New Jersey, then came to Lexington and graduated from Washington College in 1851. That same autumn, he and his brother E. D. entered Princeton Theological Seminary, graduating in 1854.

Meanwhile a vacancy had occurred at the Virginia Military Institute (VMI). Going over a list of prospective teachers, Major Hill placed his hand on the name of Thomas Jonathan Jackson. Tom felt fate had a hand in this, and as a result, the West Point graduate and veteran of the Mexican War also arrived in Lexington.

Jackson arrived in Lexington in 1851, and commenced his teaching career at VMI in the fall. The students made sly remarks about him. They laughed about his big feet. He was shy and reserved. Often in his spare time he walked to Main Street, and dropped into John Lyle's bookstore. The proprietor of the shop became a close friend. Lyle was to have a key role in leading Jackson to Dr. White and to a deeper Christian experience. But more of that later.

Perhaps Jackson's closest friend was Major D. H. Hill, a professor at Washington College. Jackson spent some of his evenings with the Hills, and later met the Morrison sisters, and escorted them when they came to Lexington for a visit.

In a small town with two colleges, there were many social functions. Dr. Junkin and his family, especially Margaret and Elinor, were invited to most of these. And at these functions the shy Major Jackson met the Junkins, and slowly developed a relationship.

Jackson went to visit the Hills almost every evening. He shared his feelings of inferiority, his problems with teaching, and keeping a step ahead of his students. Invariably his conversation strayed to speak of a certain young lady. Her name was Ellie Junkin. He was smitten. She had gotten next to him.

D. H. Hill knew Elinor well. She was charming, devout,

29

and present at most of the social gatherings in Lexington. "All of Lexington regarded her as a sweet girl, somewhat gifted in drawing, who was partially overshadowed by the brilliance of her sister Margaret's literary ability."[7]

Hill was amused at Jackson's dilemma. He seemed almost like a schoolboy. Tom said, "I don't know what has changed me. I used to think her plain, but her face now seems to me all sweetness." Tom blushed when Hill laughed and said, "You are in love; that's what's the matter."

The fact was reflected in his letters. Writing to sister Laura, he asked for the best picture available. Apparently he wanted to give it to the girl who had captured his heart. Perhaps because of Ellie, the village had captured his heart also. "I have for months admired Lexington. . . . Of all the places which have come under my observation in the United States, this little village is the most beautiful."

In his military campaigns, Jackson acted swiftly and with brilliance. However, he was unsure as to how to win Ellie. He planned his courtship with her almost as a general planned a campaign. The story would make a good Hollywood film.

Tom felt that he had a tough battle ahead. Previously young men from Lafayette College had dated Ellie. She was exposed to topflight young gentlemen by virtue of her father's position. But none had ever won her heart. Now in 1853, Ellie was twenty-eight years old. That was unusual in the mid-1800's.

The Junkin family thought that Tom was stiff, bashful, and unsure of himself. He was very polite and courteous. These virtues were seen throughout his life. Often he visited with both girls. Maggie seemed to find him intellectual. Most of the family thought he gave too much attention to little things. Later, many officers felt the same.

Like many parents, the Junkins did not realize that Ellie and the major were getting serious about each other. Naturally, in a small town like Lexington they heard the stories that made the rounds. Major Jackson was a poor teacher, rigid, but deeply honest, religious, and a good man.

30

With the passing of time, Ellie grew fonder of Jackson. Although not blind to the comments about Jackson, she overlooked them. She saw the good in him. Then for some reason, they decided to break off in the spring of 1853. However, "absence makes the heart grow fonder," and in time they were back together.

The daughter of Dr. Junkin was a pure and deeply religious girl. She was a lady with old-fashioned virtues and morals, and Tom liked that. She had a happy disposition. Some feel that later she was like an alter ego for Tom. Ellie also possessed a calm spirit with sound judgment.

Through the efforts of Mrs. Hill, time and fate, Jackson and Ellie patched up their differences, and became secretly engaged. Then came the morning of August 4, 1853. In a quiet ceremony performed at the Junkin home by Dr. Junkin, Ellie became Mrs. Thomas Jonathan Jackson.

Strangely, sister Maggie accompanied Tom and Ellie on their honeymoon. They went to West Point, Niagara Falls, Montreal, and Quebec. Tom could not wait to see the Plains of Abraham, and had a mystical experience there where Wolfe and Montcalm had battled many years before. "Tom took off his cap, as if he were in the presence of some sacred shrine. . . ." He quoted Wolfe's words after the dramatic victory, "I die content." To this Major Jackson added a postscript, "To die as he died, who would not die content."[8]

Back home in Lexington, the newlyweds went to housekeeping in a part of the Junkin home on the campus of Washington College. Tom was very proud of his wife. According to the customs of the day, his sister Laura and Ellie exchanged locks of hair.

Tom was on top of the world. He was accepted into the Junkin family as a true son-in-law. Dr. Junkin became the father that Tom had never really known. He had good relations with Ellie's sisters and brothers. However, Julia Junkin was the key to the home. She was a wonderful wife and mother. Her sudden death in February of 1854 was a great blow to Dr. Junkin and to the entire family.

From the time of their marriage in 1819, she had stood

by her husband's side as a faithful wife and helpmate. Together they had served the church in Milton, and she supported him as a college president. She was "devoted to the happiness of her family, the service of her Lord, and the interests of Zion." Wherever Julia went, she was loved and respected by all.[9]

Well read, possessed with a gentle temper, cheerful and keen of wit, she was warm and loving to her family, and to the college community in Lexington and Easton. She was like a mother to many a student. And Tom's Ellie was much like her beloved mother.

Her final message to the children was "Live near to Christ, and be kind to one another."[10] In a few words she described her own life. And these few words summarized the life of Ellie.

Julia's passing brought to an end nearly thirty-five years of harmony, confidence, sharing, and support. Dr. Junkin and his wife were extremely close. He mourned the death of his beloved companion, and sought comfort from His Lord. He and Tom spent many hours discussing the meaning of life, why we are put here, and the immortality of the soul. These discussions deepened after Ellie's death. The two men sought to comfort each other. Tom became very close to Dr. Junkin in 1854.

Even in the hour of death, Mrs. Junkin witnessed to Tom. He was still trying to persuade his sister to accept Christ. He wrote to Laura telling her about Mrs. Junkin's death:

> She without any apparent uneasy concern, passed into that unseen world, where the weary are at rest. Her life was such as to attract around her many warm friends, . . . Hers was a Christian life, and hers was a Christian death. . . . She asked us to kiss her and told her children to live near to Jesus and to be kind to one another. Her death was no leaping into the dark. She died in the bright hope of an unending immortality of happiness.
>
> My sister, Oh! that you could thus live; then might you thus die. . . . Do my sister turn to God and cast all your care on Jesus. . . . My Dear Sister, do seek religion.[11]

In the few months that she had left, Ellie witnessed to Tom as she accepted her mother's death in the faith that they would live, love, and meet again.

By the summer of 1854, Ellie was pregnant. Then an infection developed. Eight months after her mother's death, Ellie went to join her. The Lexington paper of October 26 carried this stark line: "Died, suddenly on Sunday the 22nd inst., at the residence of her father, Rev. Dr. Junkin, President of Washington College, Mrs. Eleanor [sic] Jackson, wife of Maj. Thos. J. Jackson, Professor in the Virginia Military Institute."

> Her babe and she were laid in the same grave. It was a terrible blow to the father, brothers and sisters, and especially to the gallant and godly young husband who loved her with a most intense affection.[12]

Ellie was gone, gone in the springtime of life. "I cannot realize that . . . my wife will no more cheer the rugged and dark way of life. The thought rushes in upon me that it is insupportable. . . ."

The family was shattered. Maggie had a nervous breakdown and was sent away to Philadelphia. This added to Tom's sorrow, because the two of them were very close.

Tom often wrote to Maggie, and on more than one occasion shared his heartache.

> Those days of sweet communion are gone to me. . . . Her spirit, now, and forever, will continue to bask in the sunshine of God's favor. And then to think that you and I will soon join her; that she will even meet our . . . spirits as they pass from their tenement (?) of clay, and that she will escort us to . . . Heaven. . . .[13]

At times he expressed a desire to join her. Yet his faith kept him going. She had left him monuments of God's love, and "deep dependence upon her Saviour's merits. . . . She was a child of God, and as such she is enjoying Him forever. . . ."

Tom also believed that Ellie retained all her good qualities and attributes, only in a much higher state. He often went to her grave in Lexington, but he said, "When I stand over the grave, I do not fancy that she is thus confined, but I think of her as having a gloried existence."

The Hills and Maggie were much concerned about his statements. However, it seems as though he simply had to

33

have someone who understood him, listen to his grief. When Maggie came home, Tom took a turn for the better. Precisely at 4:00 p.m. Jackson came every evening. The two of them read, chatted, and studied together. They were good medicine for each other.

Meanwhile, Dr. Junkin was struggling with his own grief, and day by day finding victory in Christ. He wrote in January of 1855, "Your sweet mother and sweet E [Ellie] are sitting in that glorious, holy society above. . . . Maj. J. [Jackson] is well, and growing heavenward faster than I ever knew any person to do. He seems only to think of E. and heaven. . . ."[14]

One of Junkin's sons writes:

> No one could, at that time, have perceived, in the modest, almost diffident, young professor of the Virginia Military Institute, the elements of high command and soldierly genius which were subsequently developed in the world renowned "Stonewall" Jackson. He appeared to be a plain, unassuming Virginia gentleman, possessed of sound judgment, good common sense, high toned honor, deep Christian humility and remarkable conscientiousness. Many sweet and pleasant hours did we spend in private Christian fellowship. The impression was left . . . that he was indeed a "devout soldier," but [young Junkin] never suspected that beneath the quiet, almost bashful exterior, there slumbered the genius and the energies of a great captain.[15]

The other members of the family stress the father-son relationship that continued between the Reverend Mr. Junkin and Jackson. He often wrote to Jackson addressing him as "my dear young son."

Meanwhile, the family was taking roots in Virginia. Young William became pastor of a church near Natural Bridge, and married a Virginia girl in 1855. The fourth son, E. D. Junkin, settled in North Carolina, became a pastor there and married a minister's daughter. In 1856, the youngest Junkin daughter married Junius Fishburn, professor of Latin at Washington College. Sadly, he died just nineteen months later. And Margaret was married to Col. J. T. L. Preston in 1857. The family was settling in Virginia and the South.

More personal sorrow loomed ahead for Dr. Junkin.

After his wife's death, he became very close to his little grandson, George Junkin Fishburn. On the fifteenth of August, 1859, little George died at the tender age of two and a half years. Dr. Junkin must have wondered what he had done to deserve all this sorrow. First a son, then his wife, then Ellie, and now the dear little boy who had been the apple of his eye.

Little George and Dr. Junkin had been almost insepar- able. "Perhaps no other trial of his life more deeply affected him." After this, the clergyman would not permit himself to get close to anyone. From this time on, he talked more and more of heaven and of things to come."[16]

He continued to write to many other pastors, and to speak out against the evils of alcohol. He was distressed at the amount of drinking creeping in among the college stu- dents. He expelled several students, and no doubt would have expelled others. However, their parents took a stand for them, and they were permitted to stay.

In the summer of 1859, and in the period after his wife's death, George found comfort in tilling the soil and tending to his 260-acre farm near Lexington.

But there were other clouds on the horizon in 1859. There was talk of war. Dr. Junkin hated the thought. He cherished the Constitution and America. He believed in rights for all. He loved both the North and the South, and felt that bloodshed could be averted if leaders went by the principles of the Constitution. He was against aggressive abolition. So his views were in line with most of the people in Virginia. Slavery should be left to the control of the in- dividual state, not the Nation. Junkin made addresses to "The Franklin Society" in Lexington along these lines.

Then came October 1859 and the John Brown Raid on Harpers Ferry. This was a blow to all moderates, and to those who advocated a calm, conservative approach. When the election of 1860 came, he was not satisfied with the platform of either major party, and cast his vote for John Bell and Edward Everett. Virginia did the same.

Virginia was upset with the election of Mr. Lincoln. Dr. Junkin started to write letters to friends in the North, urging calmness, and no rash actions to force the South to do something drastic. One letter was addressed to a young man he had known in Milton, now occupying the Pennsylvania State House, the Honorable Andrew Curtin. In the letter, he extolled the virtue of the Constitution and urged all to abide by it.

Dr. Junkin felt that secession was unlawful. "It does not break a league, but destroys the unity of a nation. To say that any State may, at pleasure, secede from the Union, is to say that the United States is not a nation."

Lincoln apparently thought along the same lines. And Junkin felt that war could be averted if the Cotton States stayed calm. Dr. Junkin's letter to Governor Curtin, dated November 11, 1860, was printed in the "Philadelphia North American."

A week later South Carolina passed her ordinance of secession, "and State after State began to move in the same direction." A convention was called in Virginia with the objective to decide where the state was going. Rockbridge County, Junkin's home area, voted ten to one to send pro Union delegates.[17]

Dr. Junkin wrote many letters to the delegates. He urged them to vote against the secession movement. He was afraid though of influence from other states. There was hope until Fort Sumter was fired upon, and Lincoln called for troops. Then Virginia, and men like Jackson and Lee, reluctantly went for the state and the rights of the commonwealth.[18]

Junkin did all he could until the very last to avert this action. In so doing, he rendered his position and life in the valley and Lexington untenable.

Several times during the month of March, a South Carolina flag was placed on the main building at the campus of Washington College, "surmounting the statue of Washington." Junkin ordered it taken down, but time and time again students put it back. He was also abused verbally, being called "Lincoln Junkin," and "a Pennsylvania Abolitionist." Slogans were written on his office door too.

On one occasion he burned the flag that had been placed

on the pole, and said, "So perish all efforts to dissolve this glorious Union."

On the fifteenth of April, his students tried to break into his classroom in an effort to get a ladder to put another flag on the pole. The morning of the seventeenth, a Southern flag was draped over Washington. He told the different classes to take it down. None listened, and Dr. Junkin resigned. He could not compromise, and would not be coerced. "I will never hear a recitation or deliver a lecture under a rebel flag."[19] Like Jackson, Junkin had his principles. The faculty supported the students since Virginia was about ready to pass an ordinance of secession. His brief note to the trustees on April 18 read, "Gentlemen, I hereby resign the office to which you called me more than twelve years ago."[20]

The trustees accepted, assured Junkin of their confidence in his integrity, and friendly regards, "for yourself and family, and our earnest prayer, that the twilight of your life may be its brightest and happiest period."

> No one can estimate the sacrifice made by Dr. Junkin in executing this decision without knowing the man, and what he was forced to leave behind. He had been happy and useful in that field of labor for thirteen years. . . . The roots of his family tree, . . . had struck deep and spread wide in Virginia soil. Three of his children, with their . . . families were left behind him, his two sons, being pastors of important churches, and married into Southern families, and his daughter, the wife of a Professor in the Virginia Military Institute. In the same institution, too, was Jackson, still dear as a son. . . .

And he had picked his burial plot in the Lexington cemetery. His wife and Ellie were buried there, as well as his little grandson.

Near Lexington was his farm, his library, and his other property. All he had near and dear were here in the valley. But in his seventy-first year, "he left it all." He left Lexington for "the love of his country, her Constitution and her flag, and returned to his native Pennsylvania. It was a crushing trial, and a heavy sacrifice; and all the more so to a heart like his."[21] He paid dearly for his stand. Sectionalism and the coming of the war brought division to his

37

household, and great sadness to his advancing years. He knew it was impracticable "for him to reside in a Southern community with his intense sentiment of loyalty to the Union."

He was given a pass from Governor Letcher, and after farewells, headed North. En route, he stopped in Winchester and talked with Mr. Logan, as we shall see in the chapter on Rev. James Graham.

Philadelphia was to be his home for the rest of his days. In the last seven years of his life, he preached seven hundred times. He worked with religious publications, visited army camps, and had a fine ministry among prisoners of war at Point Lookout and Fort Delaware. He was among the first to reach Gettysburg to minister to the wounded there.

Arriving in Philadelphia, Junkin continued to see signs of the war effort, this time from the Union side. The city was filled with the tramp of marching feet, and the rattle of drums. Everything pointed to preparation for war.

The General Assembly was meeting at the time. Junkin talked to the members, and wrote letters to the editor about the Constitution. His writings were full of political wisdom. At the time, churches were also caught up in sectionalism, and in heated discussion over states' rights.

Junkin also took time to journey to Kingston, and the old family homestead. Historically, he went there on October 31, 1861, the end of his seventy-first year, and "the beginning of the 72nd year of my sojourn in this beautiful though sin stricken world."[22]

He looked at everything that had been dear to him. At this moment, he seems to have had the eye for childhood memories, the same as Jackson had for battlefield terrain. Junkin looked at the huge rock where he fell at the age of five. Seven of the old apple trees were still there. Sadly, the old weeping willow tree was gone. The old schoolhouse, located nearby, was also gone. "I wished to tread alone the very path my feet had trodden sixty-three years ago."[23]

When evening came, he went to church. He preached from Matthew 11:28-30: "I pleaded for the conversion of some souls, as memorial to my birthday." That night, he was in and out of sleep, reliving his earlier days in Pennsylvania, the scenes of childhood, and the thoughts of those now gone.

In 1862 he preached in many churches in the Philadelphia area, and also visited his brother in Newport, Rhode Island. The brother was the chaplain of the Naval Academy. The academy had moved to Newport for safety. The air from the sea was good for him, and he enjoyed the visit very much. Dr. Junkin also had the thrill of preaching on board "Old Ironsides."[24] It was being used as a training ship at the time. He was thrilled to stand where the great sea captains had stood, and to hear the ringing of his own voice echoing through the wooden hulls.

He spent several months supplying the Canal Street Church in New York, and ministering to soldiers in the hospitals. All the time, his pen was busy writing to "maintain the authority of the government, and preserving the Union."[25]

He was very compassionate with the Confederate prisoners he met at Fort Delaware and Johnson's Island. For years after the war, the family kept the letters of gratitude from these men whom Dr. Junkin had befriended.

At Gettysburg, he met a Confederate chaplain. "And it was very touching to see the aged man of God throw his arms around the young man's neck and weep." This was an old college student.

D. X. Junkin wrote to George on May 18, 1863, confessing shock and the feeling of being stunned when he learned the news of the death of Jackson. He went to his room and wept. "I loved him dearly – but now – he is with dear, dear Ellie and the rest. . . . God comfort thee, my brother; I know He will. . . ."[26] D. X. Junkin felt that the loss of Jackson was equal to the loss of twenty thousand troops.

D. X. also shared the story of his final meeting with Jackson in Harpers Ferry in the spring of 1861. Like George, he tried to reason with Tom that rebellion and secession were wrong and inexcusable. But the time came to part.

He [Tom] held his magnificent field horse by the bridle rein. His left hand was gauntlet-gloved. He grasped mine with his right. I said, "Farewell, General; may we meet under happier circumstances; if not in this troubled world, may we meet in"–My voice failed me, tears were upon the cheeks of both, – he raised his gloved hand, pointed upward, and finished my sentence with the words – "in heaven!" And so, without another word, we parted; he mounted and rode away. . . . God comfort us and all that mourn his loss, and give us grace to secure that meeting.

Your sympathizing brother,
D. X. Junkin[27]

The war had torn asunder. And this meeting in Harpers Ferry characterizes the feeling of Jackson and the Junkin family for each other.

Junkin, meanwhile, tried to keep busy, working on theological writings. And he took up at New York. In Philadelphia, there were two institutions needing a minister. One was an Asylum for the Aged and Widows, and the other, the Magdalen Asylum, for fallen women. All who watched him were amazed at his love and compassion for the two groups of people. This period of his life was most fruitful.

A crusader, Junkin continued to write and speak out against alcohol, and against anything that would take away from Sunday being a holy day, and a day of rest. He wrote 215 pages on "Keeping the Sabbath."

To the very end, Junkin remained a student. In his seventy-fifth year, he studied Hebrews in the Greek language and left his notes of 750 pages.

Like Jackson, he did not fear death. He looked forward to the release of his spirit. Stricken on a Monday, he lingered until Wednesday. Just before his passing, he murmured several times the words "Savior" and "Heaven." Death came on May 20, 1868. He had been in relative good health until the Monday when he was stricken with a heart attack.

The funeral was held from his son's residence on Spruce Street in Philadelphia. Naturally, there were many clergymen present, and a lot of folks from Lafayette College. He was buried in the Woodland Cemetery on the banks of the Schuylkill River. His monument reads:

THE REV. GEORGE JUNKIN, D.D., LL.D.
Born November 1, 1790.
Died May 20, 1868.
"Well done, good and faithful servant."

Junkin was home at last, home on the other side with the rest of the family, including Ellie and Tom Jackson. Later he was moved to the Shenandoah Valley, to the family plot in Lexington.

Dr. George Junkin, Jackson's father-in-law. Courtesy the Presbyterian Historical Foundation

The Lee-Jackson house, the Junkin home.
Courtesy Miley Plate

III

WILLIAM S. WHITE

Hanover County, Virginia, is famous for Patrick Henry and Henry Clay. It was also the home of Samuel Davis, the founder of the Hanover Presbytery, "the mother of Presbyteries in the South and West of the United States," and from this area came William S. White.

In fact, William White's father owned Ellerson's Mill, six miles east of Richmond, which was the scene of bitter fighting in June of 1862. The family home was at Beaver Dam on the Chickahominy River in an area known as White Oak Swamp.

Father White, also named William, married Mildred Ellis in 1799, and their son, William S., was born on July 3, 1800. The baby boy was the first of seven children, four sons and three daughters born to William and Mildred.

Apparently his paternal grandmother had a profound influence on little William. She must have lived with the Whites. The Reverend Mr. White wrote later in life:

> I was carefully trained from an early age to read the word of God. This training I received chiefly from my paternal grandmother, whose maiden name was Starke. She was a woman of vigorous intellect, and eminently pious. . . .
>
> I have always believed that her bright example and faithful instructions did more to lay the foundations of my character and life than all other instrumentalities combined. She taught me to read, using a large family Bible. . . . Her plan was to turn the leaves of this Bible and teach me the large letters at the beginning of the chapters. Thus the Bible was my "first book," my only primer, spelling and reading book. . . .[1]

William slept in his grandmother's room until he was eight. In addition to reading, Grandmother White taught him to pray, and made a great impression upon him in regards to "the solemnity of the act."

In 1809, William started to the William-Henry Academy in Hanover. The school was begun under the leadership of Rev. Samuel Davies, and was fifty years old in 1809. The Reverend Mr. Hughs, an Episcopalian, was the teacher. He looked very distinguished, wearing a "coat with very broad skirts and enormous pockets, vest with flaps, . . . small white stockings, large knee and shoe buckles of pure silver, and a white flowing wig."

At noon the boys were assembled for prayer, and joined in listening to the Psalter and saying prayers. William's parents were not very religious at this stage of life. His father was a man of the world. He was wealthy, traveled a lot, ate fine foods, and socialized a great deal. He died at the age of forty-seven. His mother joined the Presbyterian Church, and apparently experienced a conversion. She outlived her husband by twenty-five years. She gave to William the gift of good common sense.

During his boyhood, a relative, the honorable Joseph M. White, came to visit at Beaver Dam. Joseph was a member of Congress from the state of Florida. He shared a word of advice with William, "Don't vegetate here on the Chickahominy. Resolve to be something."

These words meant a lot. It seems as though William was lame in one limb, causing some folks to look upon him as "that poor unfortunate child." However, William had great determination and with the words of his relative ringing in his ear, he worked hard to overcome his handicap, and reached the point where he could "outswim, outride, and outclimb any boy in the neighborhood." This was the kind of determination that would endear him to Thomas Jonathan Jackson.[2]

In the spring of 1836, the pastor of the church in Charlottesville resigned due to health and the need to be in a warmer climate. He had also served South Plains and Bethel. White was called to look the situation over, and was unimpressed. However, wise friends talked to him about the challenge and the possibility of great work in Charlottesville.

Therefore, on May 17, 1836, White commenced his work in the three churches. However, he preached but once a month in Charlottesville. The other denominations had a head start on the Presbyterians, and attendance was low.

As time passed, the folks at South Plains relinquished some of the time demanded of White. More and more he felt the field of work was in Charlottesville, the county seat.

Like most pastors, White had financial problems. He and his wife now had five children, and three of them were in school. From the time he became a father, White resolved, "that I would never attempt to make a fortune for my children; second, I would spare no expense of time, effort or money to give them a good education."

Knowing of a young student who would be good for the other churches, White asked to be released from them to devote his time and energy to Charlottesville. After much debate this was done, and White became the full-time pastor of the church in Charlottesville. He had a membership of less than twenty, and a congregation of fifty. He had a salary of $350 "and this in my eleventh year of my ministry. This seemed like receding instead of advancing."[3]

White had reason to be depressed. "I had now been preaching eleven years, and was just eleven hundred dollars poorer than when I commenced."

Until this time, White had devoted himself completely to the pastoral ministry. But now another opportunity developed, teaching school. "The school would call before me, and bring directly under my influence every day, a large number of girls . . . to which the Gospel might be fully dispensed. . . ."

White, as a teacher and as a preacher, felt responsible for the conversion and spiritual growth of every pupil and church member. He was not content with just proclaiming the word, but he sought to set a godly example. He made personal appeals to them on an individual basis for salvation. Later, he and Jackson would agree on this subject,

45

especially the idea of personal piety. And Jackson talked with General Gregg about the state of his soul after that officer was mortally wounded at Fredericksburg.

White started with twelve students, and in a year it had grown to thirty. Once again, though, it caused him financial problems. He lost two hundred dollars in his efforts to run the school. Soon he was to reap a harvest. The school grew to one hundred scholars, and a new building was erected. White had charge of the school for ten years. He states, "God was pleased to own and bless this school greatly."[4]

He continued to preach twice on Sunday at the church, conducted a midweek service, and did his pastoral visitation. There were several revivals, and in the meantime the two oldest sons were able to graduate from the University of Virginia, while his daughter completed the course of study at her father's school. The years in Charlottesville were good to the Reverend Mr. White.

The University of Virginia opened in 1824. "Mr. Jefferson brought over from Europe professors of some literary distinction, but of loose religious principles."[5] No religious worship was allowed at the university. This led to defective discipline. Thus in two years, Jefferson had to propose to the Board of Visitors that there should be a chair of theology. Later, they felt the need of a chaplain. Still morals and discipline left a lot to be desired. Robert Dabney felt the same as White about the problem.

Then on November 12, 1840, just after White became chaplain at the university, a student went to the home of Professor Davis, and started to shoot a pistol on the lawn. Dr. Davis stepped outside to see what was going on and was mortally wounded. White was with him when he died the next afternoon.

On Monday afternoon, White conducted his funeral services in the rotunda of the university. "The crowd was immense, and the grief almost uncontrollable."[6]

As a result of his death, many turned to Christ. However, problems continued. White says, "The village and neighborhood of Charlottesville had almost from time immemorial, been, not only as irreligious, but as anti-religious as any community in the State."[17] He felt as others, "that Satan had laid his thumb on Charlottesville."

Another sad experience during these years was the death of Thomas W. Gilmer, a man who had been governor of Virginia at the age of thirty-eight. President Polk had appointed Gilmer secretary of the navy. While watching the firing of a new naval gun, the Peacemaker, the weapon exploded, killing Gilmer and several others. The president barely escaped. White had Gilmer's service.

Lexington

In the summer of 1848 my social and professional life was comfortable; my school and church together afforded me a very ample support. I had purchased, enlarged and paid for a comfortable house and lot. My wife had beautified these premises with a rich variety of shrubbery. My school and congregation were full . . .; my friends kind . . . and generous; my children were progressing well. . . . I had abundant cause for contentment and gratitude. True, my labors were still heavy; my health feeble. The doctors still gave it as their opinion that I could not endure much longer the strain imposed by both preaching and teaching. . . . I had no desire to change either my home or employment.[8]

White was in the prime of life. The church and school had grown. He was well known and loved professionally and as a person. He had endeared himself to many. The church now had 140 members. He was happy. Things were fine.

However, as often happens when we get snug and comfortable, a call came from elsewhere, the call that led him to become the pastor of Major Thomas J. Jackson.

Dr. White says the call was "unexpected, surprising and painful. The decision instantly reached in my own mind was that I did not desire to go; nay, I was strongly adverse to going; it seemed to me that I could not go."[9]

As a pastor myself, I can identify with Dr. White. These things are painful. Perhaps all growth and separation is painful.

The folks in Lexington promised a salary whereby White would not have to teach. However, he loved teaching as much as pastoral work. When members of the Charlottes-ville Church heard the news, they expressed great sorrow, and all attempted to persuade him to stay. White turned to God and wrestled in prayer with the decision.

Dr. White had a challenge before him. Dr. Skinner had been at the church for seven years, and numerous problems had developed, causing a rift in the membership. A minority was for him, but the majority wanted a new pastor. So it was into this situation that Dr. White was called.[10]

In bidding his people farewell, Dr. White was unable to utter a word. "The heart was too full and too heavy for speech. Tearfully and silently I grasped the hand and turned away. To my latest breath the best of my poor prayers shall ascend [for them]."

"Next to the relation of husband and wife, parent and child, there is none on earth so tender and so sacred as that of pastor and people."[11]

The manse in Lexington was not completed, so Major J. T. L. Preston, a member of the VMI faculty, and a close friend of Thomas Jackson, offered the facilities of his home. The invitation was accepted, and in September of 1848, White started his work in Lexington. This was the same year that Dr. Junkin came to Washington College.

> The church and congregation gave me a very cordial reception. The church, . . . was larger (in size and membership) than either of those to which I had been used. The manse, just completed and never before occupied, was beautiful for situation, spacious and convenient.[12]

However, being in mid-life, Dr. White and his wife had some rough moments making the adjustment. "Old trees do not bear transplanting as do saplings. We had almost reached that period of life when persons of very strong local attachments, fond of home and neighbors, find it extremely painful to move."[13]

It's always difficult to minister before your peers. And in the Lexington congregation there were two doctors of divinity and five other Presbyterian pastors.

Like Washington College and the Virginia Military Institute, the church had historic roots. They went back to Hall's Meeting House on the banks of Whistle Creek near

Harrison's Mills, four miles southwest of Lexington. There is a possibility that a chapel was erected as early as 1745.

Rev. William Graham is the first prominent name connected with the church. In 1776 he assumed the pastorate of Timber Ridge and that of Hall's Chapel. He was also the founder of Liberty Hall, the ancestor of Washington College.

A church was begun in Lexington in 1796. It was rectangular in shape and sheltered by a large oak tree. Galleries were added from time to time. A water bucket and dipper were purchased so folks did not have to go outside for a drink.

The congregation amazed Dr. White. There were over two hundred and fifty communicants. Among them were students from the "Academy for Young Ladies, cadets of the Virginia Military Institute, and a few colored people." The townspeople filled the sanctuary on the main floor, while the girls, cadets, and blacks occupied the galleries. At times it seemed like the blacks were crowded out. To White this was an evil, and added pews were placed near the pulpit. Then more room was added.[14]

The governing body of the church at that time consisted of five trustees, twelve ruling elders, but no deacons. Dr. White soon changed the setup, and five deacons were selected. Later, Thomas J. Jackson became one of the five deacons.

One of these was John B. Lyle. He was a younger man, and the owner of a bookshop. John was a very devout man. He took his job seriously. Every day he gave some of his time to the service of the church. He kept himself posted on the needs of the congregation and the people in the area. He often spoke with people about the condition of their soul, and their relationship with God. Dr. White says, "I . . . believe that he conversed and prayed with more young men . . . than any man not in the ministry I ever knew. . . ."

White felt that Lyle was responsible for leading his two sons into the ministry. And "it was by him that I was first made acquainted with the case of General Jackson."[15]

After Jackson's arrival in Lexington, one of the places he went to most was Lyle's bookshop. There the two men became friends. Jackson confided in him, and shared his questions about Christianity.

Jackson made regular visits to the bookshop. Many people came to the store to visit and to browse. Here Jackson met many of Lexington's citizens. In those relaxed days, some of the men sang like a barbershop quartet might do today. Lyle had a great voice, and when he was not busy, led the singing. Again, Jackson appreciated this virtue and talent. John was also the choir leader at the Presbyterian Church.

Lyle found Jackson quiet and reserved, very courteous and polite. He stood very straight and stiff, almost like he was out on the drill field. He was shy, and not good in conversation and small talk.

But Lyle took him under his wing. John found, like Harvey Hill, that once you got next to Jackson, he was a pretty nice fellow. With Lyle and the Hills, Jackson relaxed and was himself.

Jackson talked about Providence and God's care with the Hills. While at Fort Washington, Tom was loosely connected with the Episcopal Church. However, as he shared with Hill about submission and surrender to the will of God, the Lord being sovereign, Hill realized that Tom's theology was along the lines of his own Presbyterian faith. Harvey, therefore, loaned him the "Shorter Catechism," and later the Presbyterian Confession of Faith. Tom studied these and found answers to some of his questions. He also appreciated the literary quality of the works.

At John Lyle's store, when the two were alone, Tom shared his feelings. He did not feel at home as an Episcopalian, but where did he belong? He was trying to live by the teachings of the Bible, but needed a church home.

Lyle was the man of the hour, the man God placed in Tom's path in the hour of his spiritual searching. John witnessed to his own faith, shared stories of how God acted in his life. Lyle was a good listener too. He permitted Jackson to talk, and then came up with a few choice observations.

As Dr. White said, when Jackson was with John Lyle, he was in good hands.

Lyle appreciated Jackson's honesty and sincerity. He shared with Tom the gamut of Presbyterian faith. Realizing that Jackson had been visiting various churches in the area in his spiritual quest, John took him to see Dr. White.

That was the beginning of a long relationship. Little did the two realize that Dr. White would later conduct Jackson's funeral service, and care for Mrs. Jackson. White and Tom had many long discussions. Tom looked upon Christian commitment as obeying the Bible to the letter. He had some mental reservations about the Scriptures, and he wondered if he could become a church member with honest doubt. After many hours of discussion with Harvey Hill, John Lyle, and Dr. White, and after much prayer, Tom took the membership vows, and became a member of the Lexington Presbyterian Church on November 22, 1851.

Dr. White and the congregation were unprepared for Jackson. Tom wanted to live as to not "violate the known will of God." He took his faith seriously, and came to confess his failures to Dr. White the same as a member of the Roman Catholic Church goes to confession. Dr. White had never seen anyone like him.

Dr. White would be amazed to find Jackson at his office door at most any hour. Tom regarded his pastor as a spiritual commander. Like a soldier on guard, he came to report any new insights, any spiritual growth, or to seek advice on problems and questions. This was added to the trips he made when he came for confession.

The Bible had to rule and govern his conduct. Hours were spent in discussing this field alone. Tom felt he had to give up dances and his slight interest in the theater. He wasn't sure there was anything wrong with all of this, but Tom wanted to "be on the safe side." When folks teased him about past conduct, he replied, "I lived, then up to all the light I had." As he looked over the difficulty of his younger days, he took a favorite verse, "We know that all things work together for good to them that love God." (Romans 8:28.) In life, in death, in the classroom, in

51

relationships, he sought to be in the will of God, in God's hands, therefore, all would turn out alright.

Mrs. Jackson reports:

> Dr. William S. White was a devout and earnest man of God, whose kindness and affability made him very winning to the young and to strangers. His impressive and persuasive style of preaching attracted and interested the new professor, [Jackson] who soon sought his acquaintance, and then his counsel in religious matters. . . .[16]
>
> Between his pastor and himself existed the most confidential relations, and he consulted him as he would a father, regarding him as a man of great worldly wisdom and discretion, as well as a faithful leader of his flock.[17]

The year 1858 brought more sorrow to Tom Jackson. During the previous year, his friend John Lyle was stricken at morning worship with a stroke and paralyzed, "and borne out of the house of God on the arms of his friends."[18]

John lingered for a year. He was able to talk to the last, and had many visitors. Among them were Tom Jackson and Dr. White. John talked to them about heaven and the glories that awaited him, and the things God had in store for all who loved Him. Tom felt that John was a living example of Romans 8:28.

Death came on July 20, 1858. Dr. White says that his sickroom had been like "the vestibule of heaven." He was a great reader, and his favorite book was the Word of God. John and Tom Jackson shared this love. White says of John, "His knowledge of the Scriptures was astonishing. He died as he had lived, the fearless, faithful servant of God."

Dr. White and Tom would both miss John Lyle. He had been their friend, confidant, and he had inspired them with his music.

> [John] not only had an ear but a soul for music. His voice . . . was inferior to none. For many years he led the church choir. He occupied the centre seat in the choir gallery, directly in front of the pulpit. The sound of his far reaching yet melodious voice, and the sight of his broad, full face, radiant with devout emotion, . . . often led me to think that his singing was as helpful to me as my preaching could be to him. . . . In his day, the singing of God's praise was a real and delightful part of the social and public worship.[19]

Such a man was John Lyle, Jackson's friend, in the faith.

Dr. White was an evangelistic preacher. In his previous church assignments, revivals had broken out, and the churches and communities were deeply touched by the power of the Holy Spirit.

Revival came to Lexington. Dr. White believed in them, "prayed for them, and was not satisfied without them."[20] He wanted the church to be alive and dynamic, a place where those who came within the doors could meet Christ, grow in grace, and experience the fellowship of the Holy Spirit with other believers.

In 1849 there was preaching or a prayer meeting every night in November. There was no television to interfere. Forty-five people met the Lord and were added to the Presbyterian Church. Others had a personal experience with the Lord, and united with other churches. There was a "sweet, sweet spirit" in the church and in the community.

In August of 1853, a revival gave new life to the church, and things continued to happen throughout the fall. Students from Washington College and VMI filled the galleries. "Much harmony and brotherly love prevailed in the church." As a result of the previous revival, the owner of the largest hotel in Lexington was converted, and promptly closed the bar.[21]

By the autumn of 1853, merchants and others were coming to Dr. White asking, "What must I do to be saved." Another forty-three souls were added to the church during this season of refreshing. Guest preachers were invited. Beverly Lacy was one of them. "The town, the College, and the Military Institute shared about equally in this blessed work."

The revivals and the pastoral work of Dr. White brought many new people to the church. Therefore, in 1857 the congregation discussed the possibility of enlarging the church. Ten feet was added to the length, and wings to the right and left of the pulpit, and the lecture room improved. The cost was $5,200. The work was completed in 1859, just on the eve of the Civil War.

By now, two Sunday schools were in operation, one for

the whites, the other for the blacks. The latter school was organized by Major Thomas Jackson in 1856. "[It] was superintended by him with distinguished energy and success. . . . The singleness of aim, the purity of motive, the enlightened zeal and practical wisdom of this man, . . . made him a blessing to the church which no language can adequately express. . . . For about ten years it was my privilege to sustain to him the two fold relation of pastor and personal friend – a privilege I shall prize as one of the richest of my life. . . ."[22]

When Dr. White came to Lexington he was sorry to see that blacks did not feel at home with his congregation. For a time, White held separate services for them on Sunday afternoon. Later, some did come and sit in the balcony.

However,

> . . . the Sabbath-school founded by General Jackson . . . was a decided success. This distinguished man threw himself into this work with all his characteristic energy and wisdom. . . . He was always punctual at the opening of the school.

Tom was no singer. He had neither the ear nor the voice, but that did not matter to the black boys and girls. Tom did the best he could with the talent he had. We can almost picture him standing before the children and leading them in one of his favorite hymns, "Amazing Grace."

Believing in reports, Tom called, in person, every month at the home of the owner of the slaves, and told the owners just how the child was doing. Once again, we see his attention to detail, and his commitment to a task. Likewise, he visited monthly the homes of his pupils. If they misbehaved, he talked the situation over with the parents. Some feel that he was a better teacher in this capacity than he was a military instructor.[23]

"Under his management this school became one of the most interesting and useful institutions in the church." Even after he went off to war, his letters contained money for the school, and he constantly inquired as to how the work was going. Despite the suffering in Lexington during the last years of the conflict, the Sunday School work in the black community continued.

Maggie Preston, his sister-in-law, writes: "When the major had become a general, and was sweeping back and forth through his native Virginia at the head of his army, he rarely wrote a letter home in which something was not said about his well-beloved Sunday School. Success or defeat, anxiety or suffering, glory or grief, nothing made him forget it, or cease to be interested in its welfare."[24]

Orders came on Saturday, April 20, for the corps of cadets from the Virginia Military Institute to report to Richmond. At supper that evening, Mrs. Jackson made some remark about preparing to leave. With a smile he replied, "My dear, tomorrow is the blessed Sabbath day. It is also the regular communion season at our church. I hope I shall not be called to leave until Monday. Let us then dismiss from our conversation and our thoughts everything pertaining to the war, and have together one more quiet evening of preparation for our loved Sabbath duties."

This was a wise decision. This was not only Jackson's last Saturday in his home with "the golden hinges," but it was to be his last night ever in his beloved Lexington. Thoughts of parting and war were pushed aside. Tom read aloud to his wife from religious magazines and newspapers. Then they turned to the Bible lesson which he was to share with the black Sunday School. When you stop to think of it, this is amazing, taking the time to prepare for his ministry on the eve of departure.

Then came Sunday morning, April 21. Jackson's footsteps would never again cross the threshold of his home or classroom. Jackson requested Dr. White to hold a brief service before he and the cadets left Lexington. White, knowing Jackson's faithfulness to time, and the order for march being set for 1:00 p.m., closed the service at 12:45. Thus, Dr. White sent Jackson off to war, and two years later received him home in death.[25]

A company of soldiers was formed at Washington College just a few days prior to Jackson's departure. Commanded by Professor Alexander Nelson, they assumed the name "The Liberty Hall Volunteers." On June 2, they were ordered to Harpers Ferry. Six days later, the company was

55

mustered on the college campus. The commanding officer was Captain James J. White, Dr. White's son.

Hugh A. White was not in the ranks at this time. Hugh was a student at Union Seminary. As his second year drew to a close in the spring of 1861, he was in a dilemma. Should he resign and enter the army, or should he remain in seminary. He was deeply troubled. On a day of fasting, he made his choice, "Our decision is formed . . . and since the war is begun, I must help finish it. It would have been more delightful to have been able to enter upon the work of saving men's souls rather than destroying their bodies."

His father urged him to finish his seminary studies and then enter the military as a chaplain. Hugh had other thoughts:

> The superior numbers and resources of the North will make it necessary for every man in the South, not disabled by age or infirmity, to take part in the work of resistance. I have thought and prayed over this question for two months . . . and the result is as a firm conviction that I ought at once to take part in the defense of my native State, and especially of you and mother, as I ever felt that I ought to preach the Gospel.[26]

To this the Reverend Mr. White replied, "Go, my son, and the blessing of God go with you."

The Liberty Hall Volunteers marched from the campus to the courthouse on Main Street. There a large crowd had assembled and presented the young men with a lovely flag. Captain J. J. White received the flag. Dr. White offered a fervent prayer in their behalf.

The townspeople escorted them to the stagecoach terminal, and then came back to the Presbyterian Church to offer more prayers in their behalf. The young soldiers spent several days in Staunton, then the Liberty Hall Volunteers entrained for Gordonsville. Then it was on to Manassas Junction and Strasburg. Then it was on to Winchester by way of wagons requisitioned from neighboring farmers. All along the route, the men from Lexington, the White brothers included, enjoyed the cheers of folks in small villages and those living by the wayside. The nearer they got to Winchester, the more the cheers intensified.

The Whites met Elisha Franklin Paxton of Lexington, a member of the Twenty-seventh Virginia. The brothers were also invited to the home of Mrs. Annie Tucker Magill, the mother of Mrs. James R. Graham. Her husband was the pastor of the Kent Street Presbyterian Church. The Liberty Hall Volunteers were incorporated into the Army of the Shenandoah as Company "I," Fourth Virginia Regiment. The Fourth Virginia was quartered at the Fairgrounds. They kidded the college men about the lack of beards and their white garters.[27]

Soon there was a fifteen-mile march in the dark to a clover field near Martinsburg. For two weeks the brothers remained at what they called Camp Stephens. It was a great experience to see the flickering lights at night, and hear the roll of drums. It was a novel sight.

The minister's son apparently adapted quite well to the military role. One day he was walking around as proud as a peacock and fell over a ledge of rocks. He hurt his leg rather badly and limped for quite a while. He was comforted by the arrival of a box of ham, beef, and pickles from home.

Hugh was taking things more seriously. He lamented the lack of proper observance of the Sabbath. True, there had been two sermons, but the soldiers were busy, cutting wood, cooking, and in some cases changing their tents. "We seek to remedy this by a brief prayer meeting held every night after roll call." Sometimes when food was short, Captain White bought rations with his own money, going into Martinsburg for coffee and other items.

Camp Stephens was located on the north side of the turnpike in a grove of trees. Jackson's headquarters were nearby in a house. However, he slept in the yard.

Captain White was burdened with military duties, and also greatly concerned about his pregnant wife. It was hard for him to concentrate on things in camp.

Then came Falling Waters. The White brothers as members of the Fourth Virginia, supported the Fifth Regiment, but were not in action. They did, however, hear the shells bursting around them and the bullets whistling around their ears.

The White brothers marched with Jackson to aid their comrades at Manassas. Shortly after midnight the Liberty Hall Volunteers halted at Paris. They were exhausted after a twenty-mile hike, and "sank prostrate on the ground." The men did not realize until daylight that they had slept in the village cemetery. Lieutenant Lyle experienced "a depression that fitted like a glove." He had slept in a sunken grave. The experience gave him the creeps.

Once again Jackson made his headquarters near the Fourth Virginia. It was Sunday, July 21, 1861. Back in Lexington Dr. White was preparing for services. And on the field of Manassas, "the thoughts of the College Boys naturally turned to home and the village church and its sacred services, and to the home folks who would spend the hours of the holy day in prayer for loved ones in the army."

This was the day of the first major battle in the east. During the height of the action the Virginians stood like a stonewall, and the commander of the First Brigade was given a new name. The Liberty Hall lads received their baptism of fire. Captain White walked back and forth in front of his men, paying no attention to the missiles flying around him.

Two days later the captain wrote to his wife:

> Sunday the 21st witnessed the most terrific battle ever fought on the continent. I lost five of my boys & have seven wounded, two of whom I fear mortally. . . . Why I was not killed is a mystery, but God in his good Providence spared me. . . . Hugh's face was black as suet; he fired twenty rounds.[28]

James was disturbed that the battle was fought on Sunday. Like Jackson, he held the Sabbath in reverence. He hoped he would never see another Sabbath like it. The only positive note was that it might bring an end to the war. The day before he wrote the letter, he prayed over his fallen men as they were about to be buried.

In those days news traveled slowly. The folks in Lexington and in the towns and villages of the Shenandoah Valley

58

awaited word from Manassas. One day shortly after the battle, a letter came addressed to Dr. White. It was from Jackson. Now thought the folks, we will learn the story of the battle. But they were surprised.

Dr. William S. White. Courtesy the Presbyterian Historical Foundation

My dear pastor, in my tent last night, after a fatiguing day's service, I remembered that I had failed to send you my contribution for our colored Sunday School. Enclosed you will find my check for that object, . . .

T. J. Jackson.[29]

The Presbyterian Church, Lexington, Virginia.
Courtesy the Lexington Church

Yet in the midst of death there was life. On July 22, Captain White received news that his wife had presented him with another child.[30]

Young Hugh had other thoughts on his mind. "Where are the souls of my dead comrades?" He made a vow to be "more zealous in seeking to win them to the Lord, so that if death came, they might sleep in Christ." For Hugh, the scenes of battle were very sad. Yet the taste of victory was sweet. "But to preach would be far better."[31]

Hugh abandoned hopes of returning to seminary for the fall session. He felt that if he survived his military experiences, he would be better fitted to serve the church. "So, if the winter is before me, I must contend with frost, and snow, and ice, instead of grappling with Hebrew roots and knotty points of theology." Hugh faced the winter alone, as James resigned from service on September 6, 1861. The resignation was due to poor health, family matters, and the insistence that he return to his teaching position at Washington College.

Hugh missed his brother as the two were very close. On the sixth of September he observed his twenty-first birthday, giving thanks for his father and his teaching. His father was his example. He never wished to be free from his father's control and advice.

Hugh's days were brightened by a visit from his father. Dr. White tells us about the visit.

In October, Dr. White journeyed east to spend some time with Jackson and the army near Centreville. Dr. Dabney says that White and Dr. McFarland arrived at nightfall, and that "Dr. White spent five days and nights with him, preaching daily." White shared morning and evening devotions with his military friend. On the last day of the visit, Jackson led the devotions. White was deeply touched.

> Never while life lasts, can I forget that prayer. He thanked God for
> sending me to visit the army, and prayed that He would own and
> bless my ministrations, both to the officers and privates, so that many
> souls might be saved. He gave thanks for what it had pleased God to
> do for the church in Lexington, . . . specially for the revivals He had
> mercifully granted to that church, and for the many preachers of the
> Gospel sent forth from it. He then prayed for the pastor, and every

member of his family, for the ruling elders, the deacons, and the private members of the church, . . . He then pleaded with such tenderness and fervor that God would baptize the whole army with His holy Spirit, that my own heart was welted with into penitence, gratitude and praise. . . .[32]

When the prayer was finished, the two stood before the fire in silence and then talked until midnight of spiritual things.

Dr. White was with Jackson when he received the order to go to Winchester and the valley. He was grateful for the trust of the country and prized that highly. On the other hand, power always leads to temptation and to problems.

When it came time to head for the valley, two other men from Lexington went with him, Colonel Preston and Sandie Pendleton.

When the news came that Jackson was going to Winchester, Hugh and the Liberty Hall Volunteers were dismayed. Hugh wrote, "No man could replace Jackson in the confidence and love of the college boys." The young men found Jackson to be open, and a man who would listen to their problems. Then came the welcome news that the First Brigade was also going to Winchester.

This time things were different. In June, it was warm and pretty girls cheered the men from Lexington. Now it was November and winter. A cold, chilly wind was blowing. After arriving in Strasburg, the men bedded down in railroad cars. Most of them forgot that it was the Sabbath, but not Hugh. When the train pulled into Strasburg, the first thing he heard was the ringing of the church bells. How he wished to obey its summons. The next morning, the troops headed for Winchester, and a bleak camp two miles south of town. Hugh was concerned about the lack of Bibles, feeling the men needed them more than "guns or powder." This letter was written on Christmas Eve.

The men received a gift on December 23. They were ordered to report to Jackson's headquarters at the north end of town. They were to be guard of honor. Thus, the company's tents were pitched on the west corner of the lawn.

The General's office was conveniently located, being the front room on the left as one entered the building, and the adjutant's general's was opposite and across the hall one sentinel guarding the doors of both offices.[33]

The tours required just one non-com and three privates at a time, so the men had time to meet the young ladies of "Glorious Winchester."

The Liberty Hall Volunteers were also very happy to have four alumni of Washington College on Jackson's staff. They were Lt. Col. W. S. H. Baylor, Captain A. H. Jackson, and Lts. A. S. Pendleton and George G. Junkin.[34]

The men were also glad for the arrival of Mrs. Jackson. Many of them had known her, and she was a warm and friendly person.

Hugh suffered through the difficulties of the Romney expedition, and then returned to Winchester until March of 1862. Spring brought another moment of decision for him. Once again he prayed about leaving the army and returning to seminary. Hugh decided to stay at his military post, temporarily abandoning "the most cherished object of his heart, the preparation for the ministry."

The spring and summer would be crucial to the South. By autumn, things would be better or worse. If better, General Jackson said he would recommend a discharge for Hugh. If worse, then it really wouldn't matter. Hugh felt it was "the duty of every Southerner to die, resisting the Northern invader."[35]

Other matters were involved. Hugh was seeing life in a new perspective. He was also distributing Bibles and religious tracts and acting as an unofficial chaplain.

A year had gone by since "King Abe ascended the throne." The fellows from Lexington thought Lincoln had done great harm. "The whole land . . . has . . . become a vast arena of deadly strife." The invaders had been made to feel the power of Virginia's strong arm. "The contest is deeping & grows daily more & more serious. Trusting in God as our deliverer, we will go forward, confidant of ultimate success."[36]

Hugh had some sad moments at Kernstown. General

Garnett, realizing that his men were about out of ammunition and in danger of being flanked, ordered a withdrawal. "We therefore retreated, loading and firing as we ran. Once, when I looked back, I saw the old Stars and Stripes waving over the ground we had just left, and this vexed me more than anything else during the day."

As he was leaving, Hugh saw one of his friends, William Bell, lying in pain on the ground. One of his hips had been broken by a musketry ball. Realizing that if he stayed he risked capture or death, Hugh left. "This is the saddest thing to do in battle, . . . leaving a wounded comrade in the hands of a cruel enemy. . . . With a sad heart I turned away to make my escape. We had to retreat under the enemy fire for half a mile. . . ." Hugh also wrote home to his father about the loyalty of the people of Winchester. Like General MacArthur, he felt sure Jackson and the First Brigade would return. In Winchester, the people cheered the captured Confederates as they were marched to the rear, and booed the Yankees.[37]

Young Hugh got a surprise in the spring of 1862. He was elected captain of the Liberty Hall Volunteers. First, James had been the captain. Now Hugh, Dr. White's other son, was the commanding officer. He turned to God for guidance, praying that "by example and effort the men of his company might become good soldiers and good Christians."

His life was now given to the military. He was not that happy with it. If spared until the end, "it will be the delight of my heart to spend the remainder of it in the ministry." But now he wanted to drive the unholy feet of the invaders from Virginia soil.

By late May Winchester was recaptured. Jackson's army received a royal welcome and feasted on things that Yankees had left behind: coffee, molasses, oranges, lemons, and figs. Many of these items the lads from Lexington had not tasted since the beginning of the war.

The Liberty Hall Volunteers still served as headquarters guard for General Jackson. Thus, they had time for reading and for the visit of friends and relatives. The military was growing on Hugh, and by mid-June of 1862 he had reached the point where he could consider staying in the service. Yet the call of the ministry was still first. Hugh urged his dad to come to the camps and bring religious literature along. Prayer meetings were still being held every night. Apparently the call to join Lee in the defense of Richmond prevented Dr. White from making this visit.

En route, Hugh was taken ill, and returned home for a few days. While recovering, Hugh wrote to brother Henry, also a Presbyterian minister, that he could not feel at ease at home while a battle was pending. Hugh also felt that God had General Jackson in his special favor "and guides him continually. Otherwise he could not run such risks in safety, and gain the most brilliant successes, when circumstances make defeat and ruin seem so inevitable."[38]

The young captain rejoined the army for the Battle of Malvern Hill. In a few days, Jackson's command moved closer to Richmond. Then Stonewall Brigade camped on the farm "of one of Hugh's uncle's in Hanover County, the ancestral home of the White's."[39]

Once again Hugh had a problem. There was a terrible shortage of ministers and many vacant pulpits. Where could he do the most good? Should He serve God in the pulpit or in the army. "If the pulpits are vacant, everything is lost." However, Hugh felt he had to stay in the army. If peace came to the Confederacy, then Hugh could complete "the cherished plan of his life to preach the Gospel." This way, he would be joining his father, two brothers, and a cousin.[40]

Hearing that his sister, Harriet McCrum, was the mother of a little girl, he turned his thoughts away from the scenes of "bloodshed and destruction to the quiet pursuits and joys of home circle."[41] Like Dabney, Jackson, and others, White felt the burden of the war had to be carried to the North, and they had to experience what Virginia was experiencing.

The end was coming, not for the Confederacy, but for Hugh. Jackson was moving against John Pope. And on August 24 Hugh wrote his last letter.

> All are as merry in camp as if the enemy was a thousand miles away. . . . This has been very little like the Sabbath. . . .[42]

Hugh wanted to seek strength and happiness from God. "With Him no storm can disturb my peace, no danger can come nigh, no harm can befall which will not do me good." This sounds like Jackson and Romans 8:28. The young officer sent one hundred dollars to the Confederate Bible Society. His last words to his beloved father were these: "You are constantly in my mind and firmly engraved upon my heart."

Then came Second Manassas. The Stonewall Brigade suffered heavily. One of those who fell was eighteen-year-old Willie C. Preston, son of Jackson's teaching colleague at VMI and his brother-in-law by his first marriage. When Jackson heard the news he walked off to be alone. That night a prayer meeting was held. Chaplain Hopkins and others tell us about it.

Colonel Baylor, acting commander of the Stonewall Brigade, sent a message to Captain White, proposing the prayer meeting.

> I know the men are very much wearied out by the battle of today, and that they need all the rest they can get to fit them for the impending struggle of tomorrow; but I cannot consent that we shall seek repose until we have had a brief session of prayer, to thank God for the victory of today, and to beseech His continued protection and blessing during this terrible conflict.[43]

As the fighting raged the next day, Colonel Baylor grabbed the flag of the Thirty-third Virginia and rushed forward at the head of the brigade. He fell mortally wounded. At that moment, Hugh White grabbed the colors and waved them in the advance of his company. While urging his men on, he too fell, hit by an enemy bullet and dying instantly.

Jackson had looked upon Hugh as the ideal Christian soldier. He had lived his faith in the military. He was often found distributing religious literature. Jackson said "Though his loss be mourned, yet it is gratifying to know he left us a bright example and that he fell, sword in hand cheering on his men, and leading them to victory in repelling the last attack of the enemy upon that bloody field."

To Dr. White, Jackson wrote:

> The death of your noble son and my esteemed friend Hugh, must have been a severe blow to you, yet we have the sweet assurance that, whilst we mourn his loss to the country, to the church, and to ourselves, all has been gained for him.[44]

Young James Smith writes:

> Dear Hugh, the purest, the truest, the best of all. . . . What a blessed ministry we did anticipate in his! How full of promise, of usefulness were his amiable, attractive qualities, his accurate and increasing attainments, and his quiet, yet earnest, active piety.[45]

Lt. Givens B. Stickler, Hugh's successor, exclaimed, "How rare are such characters."

The writings of Dr. White sound much like those of Jackson.

> God has been a present help to me in trouble. Even in the death of my son, slain in battle, who was all that a son could be to his father and mother, I have had a very sweet experience of God's great goodness in giving him to us, in making him what he was, and in taking him to himself just when and as he did. I firmly believe that he had fulfilled the allotted measure of his days, that he had accomplished his mission, and answered the end of his being. He ardently desired to preach the Gospel, but his will was to do and suffered the will of God.[46]

Earlier Hugh had expressed his feelings about the war and about suffering by saying, "He will certainly bring light out of this darkness and joy out of this sorrow. Weeping may endure for a night, but joy cometh in the morning."

Dr. White shared his grief with Dr. Brown, writing on September 6:

> My son Hugh is in heaven. His body perished on the plains of Manassas, on the 30th of August. . . . I can learn nothing of the particulars, except that he was killed instantly. General Jackson's adjutant writes merely this: "Hugh was killed in the battle of Saturday. He fell gallantly leading his men. I sincerely sympathize with you in the loss of a son so faultless as a Christian and a soldier. . . ."
>
> His redeemed soul is safe, and I look up through my tears, and in that rejoice.

In one of Hugh's last letters to his parents, he shared his commitment:

> I feel more and more deeply that I must live altogether for God and in God. . . .[47]

Even with his faith, Dr. White naturally experienced a parent's grief. He writes:

> The remnant of my pilgrimage on earth is rendered far more lonely by his early death. But this remnant is brief, and its termination will bring me into joyful and never ending communion with him and many others who have gone before.

Jackson's pastor continued by saying:

> My own congregation and my own family became . . . deeply involved in this mighty struggle. The invading forces were already on the march upon our northern border. Thirty five communicants of my church and thirty members of my congregation, not communicants were soon in the ranks and on the weary march to meet the foe. . . .

They were the first of many. By the autumn of 1864, the Lexington Church gave 106 officers and men to the Confederate war effort. In that same period, eighteen of that number were killed, another five died of wounds or disease, and five were disabled by wounds.

Among those killed were William C. Preston, and his own son Hugh at Second Manassas, and Generals Jackson and Paxton at Chancellorsville.

Not only were his own sons away at war, he was involved in ministering to the members of the church and community when bad news came from the front. And he was called upon to have the services for many of those killed in action when they were returned to Lexington for burial.[48]

One of his sad moments came at the funeral of General Jackson. The general's wife writes:

> At Lexington our pastor, Dr. White, and our friends and neighbors met us in tears and sorrow.[49]

On Friday, May 15, Jackson's service was conducted from the Presbyterian Church, with Dr. White presiding.

The man whom Jackson looked upon as his spiritual commander read from 1 Corinthians 15. And after the services, the Whites took care of Anna for several days.

After Gettysburg, it was all downhill for the Confederacy. When the Army of Northern Virginia reached Winchester, many citizens joined them and headed south. Cornelia McDonald was one of them. She has left an epic description of life in Lexington during the last twenty-one months of the war.

Dr. White had his memories too. And they were sad ones.

> In June, 1864, the enemy, twenty thousand strong entered the quiet village of Lexington. General David Hunter was in command, a man whose notoriety among our people made him terrible to the timid and detestable to all. . . .[50]

Hunter seemed to glory in the suffering he could bring to women and children. He watched with glee as his men tramped through nice homes, taking what they wished, spilling personal items on the floor, vandalizing the place and terrifying the residents. When helpless women protested, he replied, "These are the brutal consequences of war, and you must bear them as best you can."

By Hunter's orders, a June Sabbath was spent in robbing and then applying the torch to the home of Governor Letcher in Lexington, two homes belonging to professors at the Virginia Military Institute, the spacious barracks on the Institute, a large flour mill, and a warehouse belonging to the state of Virginia.

VMI "was robbed of its library, of its splendid paintings, and . . . a bronze statue of General Washington. . . ." The superintendent's house escaped destruction only because his daughter was very ill.[51] "This residence is now all that remains of that once beautiful establishment – barracks, professors' houses, mess hall, hospital, and offices are all in ashes." Hunter had applied the torch.

Washington College was also sacked, the library and lovely paintings carried off. The furniture from the school was either hauled away by the soldiers, given to the local blacks or destroyed. All the windows were broken, and

Hunter was ready to apply the torch. However, a gray-haired trustee talked him out it.

Lexington was shelled before Hunter entered. Twenty homes were struck, some were damaged, and two caught fire. Six shells passed over Dr. White's home. One exploded in the garden, and another in the stable yard. Union soldiers took five hundred dollars worth of corn and hay from Dr. White. Some of his harnesses were also stolen. Only the efforts of a sergeant assigned by General Averill to guard the manse prevented the stealing of White's carriage. And poor old "Charley," White's favorite horse, "one I had used under the saddle for nine years—a horse almost as well known through Rockbridge County as his owner," was stolen. This made Black John exclaim to Dr. White, "These Yankees are the beat of all the rogues I ever saw, black or white."[52]

General Averill attempted to halt such acts. He dealt strongly with men under his command who entered private homes. He was too much of a gentleman to remain long under Hunter. White told him "politely, but firmly, that my principles and sympathies were all with my native South." White was able to move along the troops without insult or threat of bodily danger.

White was amazed to find no services being held on the Sabbath. He asked if there were no chaplains. A major answered, "O yes, we have a great many, almost one to every regiment [but] they are not of much account." The major stated that he had not heard a sermon or prayer for months. This was in marked contrast to conditions in Jackson's command.

One chaplain was seen standing in front of the Letcher mansion, and laughing while it burned. Near him stood Mrs. Letcher and her children on trunks, in great dismay over the flames taking away their precious home.

Dr. White was glad that General Averill pitched his headquarters tent in the yard of the manse, "within forty feet of my study door, and his signal corps encamped in my garden."[53] This was a great protection for the house, but did not help the stable and carriage house.

White felt that with a man like Hunter at the head of the army, that Lexington and its twenty-five hundred inhabitants were fortunate to get off as well as they did. His thought was, "May it please God soon to terminate this cruel and unnatural war."

The preacher then stated that his views were like those of Jackson. "I was not a secessionist, but a rebel, an honest, earnest rebel." When the president "called for Virginia bayonets to impale the bodies of our nearest neighbors and dearest friends, the time for rebellion with a view to revolution seemed to me to have come."[54]

In a few days General Early arrived. His veteran troops scared Hunter, marched by Jackson's grave, swept on to Winchester, levied a $200,000 ransom on Frederick, and swept on to the gates of Washington. President Lincoln stood on the ramparts to watch their deployment. However, Mr. Lincoln and U. S. Grant wanted to insure that this type of threat would never happen again.

Phil Sheridan was given command of the Army of the Shenandoah. In September 1864 came the third battle of Winchester, Fisher's Hill, and Cedar Creek. And that brought the burning when Sheridan applied the scorched earth policy. The granary of the Confederacy was burned, mills, barns, and crops went up in smoke and flame.

Alexander Swift Pendleton, better known as Sandie, and the son of Rev. William Nelson Pendleton, fell at Fisher's Hill. Thus both clergymen had given a son to the cause. Each had served under Jackson.

Despair was everywhere. Morals hit the bottom. To escape from the disaster of war, many pious people turned to alcohol. Long an advocate of the temperance movement, White lamented what was happening.

Yet there was scarcely a home where death had not come. A son, father, or sweetheart had fallen on some battlefield, and now there was sadness, and a vacant chair. Or with the doctors away in the military, aged and children died from the lack of medical care. The winter of 1864-65 was extremely dark in Lexington.

Food and clothing were very scarce. Prices were outrageous, Confederate currency was worth little. In fact, after the war, the Reverend Mr. Pendleton's family survived largely due to the gifts of food and clothing from former parishioners in Frederick, Maryland.

During all this time, Dr. White was wondering whether or not his other two sons would survive the war. He had already lost one. He hated the thought of losing another.

One young son was brought home in November, badly wounded. He had been hit by seven balls on Rude's Hill near New Market. One had hit his left calf and done a lot of damage.

Mother and Dad White hoped that he would stay home and not return to war. On April 10 came the news that the same son had been captured on April 2. For several days there was no more word of either son.

Then on April 15, both boys returned home. It was 1865. The war was over. They had survived. Dr. White states his feelings:

> Our brave and honored army, overborne by vastly superior numbers and utterly exhausted by continued marching and fighting without food or rest, has been compelled to surrender. Our capital and commonwealth are now under the heel of our enemy. . . . We are . . . a subjugated power, ruined as to all political power, . . . But these things are not paramount. We have other relations than political. I am a husband, father, minister of the gospel, as well as citizen of the State. If our social and religious privileges are not denied us we can endure all else. . . . Our blessed Lord can surely do more to make his people permanently happy than men and devils can to make them miserable. . . .
>
> The fearful struggle of four years has ended. The work of carnage and death is over. Forced back into a position from which we sought to escape, the mortified victims of a power which we have hated, I bow reverently to God. . . . I make no further record of these sad times, except to express my deep and painful apprehensions for the future destiny of the negro and my own descendants. . . .[55]

White was now sixty-five years old. He was in poor health, and he thought there was "little of earthly ill to fear or of earthly good to expect." He hoped his time was near. And his time was short. However, he would still make some fine contributions of time and service to the people of Lexington and the South. He shared in a big moment. On

October 2, 1865, Robert E. Lee was installed as the president of Washington College. Dr. White had a "fitting and impressive prayer." He tied in with Lee's feelings by praying for the president of the United States.

After the war, White resumed his friendship with another *preacher Jackson knew.* William Nelson Pendleton, the West Point graduate, and former commander of the Rockbridge Artillery returned home from the war. Pendleton, like White, had lost a son. Alexander S., better known as Sandie, was one of Jackson's favorite staff officers. Like Hugh White, he too contemplated entering the ministry after the war. One of the delights of the winter of 1863 was Jackson watching the romance bloom between Sandie and Kate Corbin at Moss Neck. Soldiers in the ranks debated which one prayed the most, Jackson or Sandie. Now no doubt these two preachers shared their sorrows.

They were joined by a newcomer at the Baptist Church, John William Jones, whom we have already met. In October of 1870, the three preachers had a sad task. They shared in the funeral services for Robert E. Lee. Sorrow had invaded their ranks, and the streets of Lexington once again.

On November 2, 1866, health problems which had been bothering White "for more than two years have at last resulted in a total suspension of my ministry. . . . I have been compelled to retire from the pulpit."

Dr. White had throat problems. He had been preaching for thirty-nine years, without any kind of amplification. Like any minister, he had used his voice a great deal. Everything was fine until near the end of the war, then he developed a cough and hoarseness. He found great difficulty in speaking, and often his voice just faded away.

Accordingly, he submitted his resignation, effective January 1, 1867. It was declined, and the governing body of the church gave him a leave until that date, continuing his salary, providing a substitute, and caring for him, hoping for his complete recovery. He was overwhelmed, and the tears flowed because he was so grateful.[56]

However, his health did not improve that rapidly. And

on March 9, 1867, he again tendered his formal resignation. On April 13, 1867, it was accepted. Many in the congregation did not want to accept it, and trouble threatened. But Dr. White said it was best. He had come to Lexington in 1848. Now his work was ended.[57]

Perhaps the release from responsibility helped, or maybe it was the rest. Anyway, by July, White's voice had improved, and he was able to do some pulpit supply. The Ann Smith Academy for girls also needed a teacher. So he and Mrs. White accepted this ministry. He and Jackson always felt that they should do their best. White threw himself into the work with the same vigor as he did in Charlottesville, twenty years earlier. He also continued to write for periodicals, and kept up a prolific correspondence. All of this proved to be too much for the old soldier of the cross, and his health broke.

It was very touching to see

> two old people, who had spent their whole life in the service of God in the church, broken in fortune, enfeebled by age, of their own accord stepping down from prominence and competency, declining to live with their children because as they often said, "if they could not help, they would not hinder" them, and going into the school-room to earn their bread "by the sweat of their brow."[58]

The Whites wanted to be active and useful to the last. They counted it a joy to be doing something, and they had a lot to offer. For three years Dr. and Mrs. White taught at the school. His resignation was accepted on August 3, 1871. The trustees were profoundly grateful for his services. They knew it would be tough to replace him. Affectionately they said, "[We] pray that your honored and useful life may be long spared in the midst of this community, where the marks of your abundant labors are everywhere visible."[59]

White heard the voice of God calling "him out of the struggle to unbuckle his harness and be still." His voice was gone again. He could not speak. But he could write. And in this period he wrote the "Notes" which became the source of the book about his life and ministry.[60] And he was taken by his doctor and friends to cast his vote for his friend, General Kemper, who was running for governor. He was a Christian, a family man, and a Virginian to the core.

Giving up his beloved Lexington, he went to the home of his daughter, Harriet McCrum. On November 29, 1873, he passed over the river to join Jackson and his son Hugh.

IV

JAMES GRAHAM

James Robert Graham was born at Montgomery, New York. This is in New York State, north of New York City, and near the Hudson River. His birthday was July 15, 1824. He was the son of William G. and Hannah Houston Graham.[1]

James attended Union College, Schenectady, New York, graduating in 1844. Six years later he graduated from Princeton Theological Seminary. He was licensed to preach by the Hudson Presbytery, and ordained on October 9, 1851. He made his way to Winchester, and from 1851 to 1900 served as pastor of the Kent Street Presbyterian Church.[2]

This church had come into being on November 15, 1825, when five men bought the southern half of Lot Number 107 in the Fairfax Addition, at the northeast corner of Kent and Boscawen streets. This is the present site of the *Winchester Evening Star*. The congregation became a part of the Winchester Presbytery on June 27, 1827. This church was to become Jackson's church during the Civil War. In 1900 the Kent Street Church merged with the Loudoun Street Church.

Living in Winchester at the time was Dr. Alfred T. Magill. He was a general practitioner and then a teacher at the University of Virginia. He married Ann E. Hunter Tucker on November 1, 1827. Their home was built by Judge Tucker, Ann's father. It stood on North Market Street. Here on December 17, 1828, a daughter, Fanny, was born. Here the young Presbyterian preacher, James

76

Graham, courted her. They were married on October 3, 1853. Fanny was twenty-five years old at the time.

To this union eight children were born, three of whom became ministers. They were Alfred Thurston, June 4, 1858; Henry Tucker, August 21, 1865; and James Robert, Jr., October 19, 1863.

On January 1, 1855, the trustees of the Kent Street Church purchased a large brick house at 319 North Braddock Street from Lewis Lauck. This property was the first and only manse or parsonage for the Kent Street Church. This was home of Dr. and Mrs. Graham until the preacher's death.

Of the ministerial sons, Alfred graduated from Hampden-Sydney in 1878, and Union Seminary five years later. He served in Rockville, Maryland, from 1883-89, Davidson, North Carolina, 1889-1907, and then one year in Lexington, Virginia.

James was ordained to Foreign Mission work on June 5, 1889. He sailed for China and had a long and distinguished career in the Orient. Henry Tucker Graham also became a missionary. He spent five years in Japan, and then served pastorates at Fayetteville, North Carolina, and Farmville.

John Randolph became a doctor and practiced in New York City. One daughter, Evelina Tucker Graham, seems to have remained home and took care of her father after Mrs. Graham died on May 13, 1901.

The Reverend Mr. Graham had an unusual introduction to Thomas J. Jackson. Strangely, it was by another Presbyterian minister, Tom's former father-in-law. Graham tells how it happened:

> I never knew there was such a man . . . till about the time hostilities commenced. One evening, late in April, I dropped into Mr. Logan's store and found him unusually excited. . . . He had just had a call from Rev. Dr. George Junkin, late president of Washington College, Lexington, Va. The old doctor had been an able and distinguished president of the college for about a dozen years, and was the father of General Jackson's first wife. In the stormy discussion which preceded the war, he, with most of the prominent men of Lexington, including General Jackson himself, warmly espoused the cause of the

Union; . . . when the rupture came, . . . almost, if not all, of the others cast their fortunes with the Confederacy. . . .[3]

Mr. Junkin was not in that group. He remained loyal to the Union, and decided he could not stay in Lexington. Therefore he headed north to Pennsylvania, and stopped in Winchester en route.

While resting their horses . . . he called on Mr. Logan, and in answer to inquiries as to why and where he was traveling, he said with characteristic vehemence, "I am escaping from a set of lunatics. Lexington is one vast madhouse. There is not a sane man there, nor woman either. . . . I am compelled to leave the best friends a man ever had. I leave most of my children too, and my son-in-law, Major Jackson, who is the best and bravest man I ever knew, but he is as crazy as the rest. Yet if there is to be a war, as I fear, I tell you, now, that Major Jackson, if his life is spared, will be among its most distinguished heroes."[4]

This prediction made a strong impression upon Graham. He remembered the name and before the year was over, he was to meet the crazy and brave Major Jackson, now a general in the Confederacy.

First, though, came the news of Jackson at Harpers Ferry, and then the dramatic story of Manassas and account of the First Brigade, men of the Shenandoah Valley standing like a "Stonewall." And in early November, Tom Jackson returned to Winchester as commander of the Valley District.

The following Sunday he was present at Graham's church, accompanied by Colonel Preston, a member of his staff, and a former teacher and founder of the Virginia Military Institute.

From that moment, whenever Tom was near enough, "he was a regular attendant upon our services."

January 1, 1862, brought a new year, and a new experience for the Reverend Mr. and Mrs. Graham. This was the day Jackson started his ill-fated Romney campaign. Mrs. Jackson had arrived in Winchester about two weeks earlier, and had stayed at the Moore house with him. But now Tom was leaving, and he did not know when he might be back to Winchester. Someone had to look out for his wife. But who? Perhaps a minister, and what minister would be better than a Presbyterian. Thus, the choice fell to the Reverend Mr. and Mrs. Graham.

After the troops had started for Bath, now Berkeley Springs, Tom went to the manse, "and asked, as a great favor, to receive Mrs. Jackson and take care of her for a few days while he would be absent from town. . . ." Tom said she was a minister's daughter, and a stranger in town. He would be greatly pleased if they would take care of her.

The Grahams could not say "no." Within an hour he brought Anna to the manse, and then was off with his staff, riding the road to Bath. When he returned three weeks later, he asked if it might be possible for him to stay with his wife at the Grahams.

There was a joyful reunion that evening in late January when he returned to the Presbyterian manse and his wife. He had ridden over muddy Virginia roads throughout the day, gone to his headquarters to clean up, and then came to the Grahams. Mrs. Jackson describes the moment.

> He came bounding into the sitting room as joyous and fresh as a schoolboy, to give his wife a surprise. . . . As soon as the first glad greetings were over, . . . with a face all aglow with delight, he glanced around the room, and was so impressed with the cosy and cheerful aspect of Mr. Graham's fireside, as we all sat around it, that winter evening, that he exclaimed: "Oh, this is the very essence of comfort!"[5]

Dr. Graham held Jackson in high esteem:

> No man has lived in this generation, if in any that preceded it, whose personality has awakened such profound and widespread interest. . . .

Although there were other great figures in the War Between the States, "He was . . . the most conspicuous figure it produced." In Graham's estimation no other leader generated the enthusiasm which "his career excited, or in the admiration which his achievements called forth."[6] Stuart may have been more dashing, but Jackson was the one with whom the rank and file of the people and the military could most easily identify.

79

Twenty years after Jackson's death, people in Britain and in the United States were still talking about his character and career. Graham knew this from personal observation, and we know it 120 years later.

Graham, in sharing his recollections of Jackson, says:

> It is an old proverb that "you must live with a man to know him thoroughly." I lived with him [Jackson]. For about two months he slept every night under my roof and sat every day at my table, and bowed with us every morning and evening at our family altar. He called MY house his HOME.[7]

In thinking of the two months they spent together, Graham saw a real Christian spirit and witness in Jackson. They had no disagreeable moments, even though there were two families under the same roof. He was cheerful, and considerate, and contributed to the happiness of the household on Braddock Street. "To the last [Jackson had] cordial relations with every member of the household—parents, children and servants. . . . No man could have been more considerate or congenial." Dr. Graham heard about Jackson having peculiar ways. However, the clergyman looked for and tried to find some. He had no luck. Maybe that was because they were such close friends.[8]

In social gatherings in Winchester, Jackson was kind and pleasant. "He met at my table and fireside a great many people [from all walks of life] and of both sexes, and to all of them he was . . . cordial."[9] If a young enlisted man came to the Graham's for dinner and seemed to feel ill at ease in the presence of the general, Jackson did everything possible to make him feel at home.

One of the things that Graham did notice was Jackson's methodical ways. He rose at a certain hour, always early, went at once to headquarters nearby, and a few minutes before eight o'clock, returned for breakfast. His wife knew just when to expect him. In fact, one could set his watch by Jackson's activities. "In not a single instance, I believe, was the meal delayed so much as one minute by his failure to appear on time. If something did come up detaining him at the office, he sent word."[10]

The general never brought the cares of war and command to the table. He would not discuss military matters at home. He conversed about many things, and was normally cheerful. "He was a good listener." Occasionally after dinner he would talk about enemy movements. However, he covered only what was generally known, and already covered in the press.

One day a Winchester lady asked him a direct question. Jackson had an answer, "Mrs. − − −, I'll have to say to you as the school boys sometimes say, 'Ask me no questions, and I'll tell you no lies.' " His sense of humor came through in that moment, and many times during the winter of '62.

If couriers came to the Graham home, they were directed to go to headquarters. The Reverend Mr. Graham said that was unnecessary, and offered his own study. Jackson promptly answered, "No, sir, this is a private house, and my men must learn that no official intrusion can be allowed."

Sometimes after dinner he would converse about Union leaders. Many of them he had known from his days at West Point, or in prewar service. He held McClellan in high regard, and said, "If he can handle his troops in the field with the same ability with which he organizes them in the camp, he will be simply invincible."[11]

Jackson shared with the Winchester cleric the view that "War means fighting. . . . Armies are not called to dig trenches, to throw up breastworks, and lie in camps, but to find the enemy and strike him, to invade his country and do him all possible damage in the shortest possible time." This sounds like the modern purpose of the infantry to search for and destroy the enemy. In Jackson's eyes, an army must "move swiftly, strike vigorously and secure all the fruits of victory." This was the secret of "successful war."

Graham tried to get an opinion from Jackson about First Manassas. The general had little to say. However, Graham got the feeling that had he been in command, the army would have headed for the grounds of the Capitol in Washington.

The second major virtue that Graham saw in Jackson

81

was that of self-control. He always seemed to be in control of himself and situations. Even during the trouble over the Loring letter, Jackson relaxed and talked freely of his travels to Europe. Graham was amazed at his serenity of spirit. He was the living example of the verse, "Better is he that ruleth his spirit than he that taketh a city."

Jackson believed in divine providence. Therefore, he trusted God. He believed Romans 8:28 to be true. He was simply an instrument in the hands of the Almighty. General Taylor and others have alluded to the fact that even when riding he seemed to be praying, or in meditation before a campfire. "Those who rode or walked beside him on the march have told me [Graham] that they often saw his lips moving as if in silent prayer. Before he went into battle he might be found upon his knees. . . . And when the battle was over, he always recognized it not by his own skill or valor, but by the favor of the Almighty Ruler of whom he had asked the victory, and to whom he bowed again in humble thanksgiving for the victory that had been granted."[12]

Dr. White, the Reverend Mr. Ewing, and others have spoken of his power in prayer. Graham also saw it. "No man ever evinced more of the spirit of prayer, and not many have had such gifts in prayer."[13]

November 15, 1861, was appointed a day of fasting and prayer for the Confederacy. Jackson had just arrived in Winchester. Dr. Graham held a service, and during the singing of the first hymn, General Jackson walked into the Kent Street Church. A little later, Graham asked, "Will General Jackson lead us in prayer?"

The request came as a surprise both to Jackson and to the congregation. But after a pause, Jackson arose, and "led us at once to the presence of God and to the throne of Grace." Pouring out his soul before God in a simple childlike manner, "he besought God to bless our afflicted country and give success to our arms." He prayed for mercy and for God to be gloried. Like Dr. White a few weeks earlier, Dr. Graham never forgot the prayer, nor the spirit with which it was uttered. "It seemed to teach men how to pray in troublous times."[14]

Two big events in the relationship between Jackson and the Grahams occurred at a time of parting. The first came when Jackson had to leave Winchester in March of 1862, and the last at their final farewell in November of the same year.

On March 11, Patterson and the Union army was advancing in force. Major Harman had removed all the army stores and sent them to Mount Jackson. Colonel Ashby was playing hide-and-seek, and hit-and-run with the Union advance.

When dinner came, the Grahams felt that Jackson would be unable to come. Mrs. Jackson had left several days earlier. "But he came to supper and, to our surprise, all aglow with pleasant excitement, because of the splendid behavior of his troops and their eagerness to meet the enemy." Some ladies came in and were in deep gloom over the situation. He did not try to deny the reality of the situation, but with his cheerful, positive manner, gave them hope.

Jackson stayed for evening devotions. He seemed in no hurry to leave. Apparently he was trying to reassure the folks he had come to love so much. After all, they were fearful over the thought of the retreat of the Confederate army. When he did go, he said, "Oh, I'll see you again." Then he added, "I don't expect to leave."

But things were happening of which Jackson was unaware. His officers had set the column in motion for a movement to the rear. Jackson had planned to launch a surprise counterattack under the cover of darkness.

About an hour later Jackson returned. The Grahams were not home. A servant was sent to find Mr. Graham with the message that Jackson wanted to see him at headquarters.

> Hurrying there, I found him walking the floor under more excitement than I had ever seen him exhibit before. He had undergone in the brief space of time a surprising change. His countenance betrayed deep dejection, and his spirit was burdened with an inexpressible weight of sadness.

Like many others in grief, Jackson did not know what to say. When he composed himself, he stated that he had not meant to deceive the Grahams and his friends. He did not want to abandon the town. It was like a second home to him. "He had intended to lead his troops out that night, and hurl them on the camp of the enemy, and drive such as were not captured and might survive back to the Potomac."

He laid the plans before his officers, but they felt the attack would not work. Jackson again paced the floor, grabbed the hilt of his sword, his face was blazing, "I may execute my plan yet." Graham was awed by his presence. The fire of battle had returned. Then in calm assurance he said goodbye to Graham and expressed the hope that "a good Providence would permit him soon to return and bring deliverance to the town."[15]

As the army retreated, he told Dr. McGuire that he would never hold another council of war. And he didn't. Jackson was back at Kernstown in a few weeks, and then delivered the town in May of 1862.

Like the rest of the folks in Winchester, the Grahams were very happy to learn of the advance of Stonewall's army on Sunday, May 25, 1862. They heard the sounds of battle as it raged on the heights near Handley High School. They saw the Union troops under General Banks falling back, headed for Martinsburg. They must have been overjoyed.

Late in the evening they heard footsteps on the porch of the manse. They sounded familiar. Sure enough, it was General Jackson coming to see his old friends, on the day he had cleared the valley, and freed his beloved Winchester.

Throughout the summer, letters flowed from Mrs. Graham to General and Mrs. Jackson. The Reverend Mr. Graham, to help meet expenses, opened a school in the basement of the manse.

The Reverend Mr. Graham had an interesting experience in the autumn of 1862. General White and the Union soldiers blew up the Ammunition magazine at Fort Garibaldi. The people had been warned that the destruction was coming. He went up on the roof several times to look toward the location and pray. Then came the explosion. It occurred while he was on the roof. He saw the hill lift up into the air. He said the house rocked, almost like being hit by an earthquake. A few windows were broken by the blast. The clergyman never forgot his eyewitness experience.[16]

Cornelia McDonald was in church on a Sunday in November 1862. Jackson had spent October at Bunker Hill, and then moved his headquarters to the Berryville area, and then back to Winchester. By mid-November, he was close to the Grahams again.

Mrs. McDonald describes the Sabbath at the Kent Street Presbyterian Church: "He listened very closely to the sermon, and had on a splendid new uniform. He looked so serene and modest. . . . In one short year his fame had spread over the world, and now he was looked upon as a great Captain."[17] This was November 16.

The Reverend Mr. Graham describes the famous Winchester portrait, the one Mrs. Jackson said was her favorite. The general, Dr. McGuire, and another staff member had ridden to Winchester. The commander took dinner at the home of Dr. Hugh McGuire, just south of the Reverend Mr. Graham's. The clergyman was one of the invited guests.

During the course of the meal, fourteen-year-old Betty McGuire suggested that Jackson get his picture taken. He said little, but later left in secrecy, and apparently got a haircut. Then he went to comply with the little girl's wishes.[18]

On the night of November 21, Mrs. Graham took time to write to Mrs. Jackson who was about ready to give birth to the child conceived the previous winter in Winchester.

She related that Jackson had taken his headquarters in Winchester on the nineteenth. Dr. Graham went to see him on the twentieth. By the morning of the twenty-first, some elements of the army were on the move again, and Grahams feared they would not get to see the general. Jackson came to tea and the old friends had a fine time. It seemed like old times.

... those cheery old times of last winter; we were all so cosy in our dining room and around the table we did wish for your seat between us. Indeed, the presence of your dear little self was all that was wanting to complete the pleasure of the evening. He is looking in such perfect health ... and is in such fine spirits. ... We did enjoy him to the full.

The children begged to be permitted to sit up to see "General Jackson," and he really seemed overjoyed to see them. ... I have no doubt it was great recreation for him. He seemed to be living over last winter again, and talked a great deal about the hope of getting back to spend this winter with us, in that old room, which I told him I was keeping for you and him.[19]

The general told Fannie he expected to be leaving in the morning, but hoped to get back. Fannie spoke of all the adulation he had received. Yet Tom "is the same humble, dependent Christian, desiring to give God the Glory, and looking to Him alone for a blessing. ... I always feel assured that he does everything under the guidance of our Heavenly Father, and this is the secret of his wonderful success."[20]

Fannie took time to prepare him a lunch for the morrow. Then they went to the family altar and prayed. Tom prayed for the Grahams and for his wife, and for God's will to be done, no matter what happened. Then they parted. Tom headed east for Fredericksburg, Moss Neck, and Chancellorsville. The Grahams and Tom were never to meet again on earth.

Graham enjoyed cordial relations with most of the Union officers in occupied Winchester. However, during the winter of 1863, Milroy's occupation, the manse was subject to searches on several occasions. Union authorities thought Graham might be hiding Confederate spies. The entire house was subject to search, basement to attic. On one occasion, Jackson's Winchester pastor was arrested.

Jackson's widow and the Grahams remained friends long after the war. Mrs. Jackson and her daughter visited the Grahams several times.

Although he supplied the Falling Waters, Tuscarora, and Gerrardstown Presbyterian churches, his only parish was that of the Kent Street Church in historic Winchester.

The Reverend James Graham. Courtesy the
Frederick County Historical Society

Forty-nine years, from October 9, 1851, to March 20, 1900,
was spent as the pastor of that church.

During the difficult days of the Civil War, he was principal of a school in Winchester, giving it up in 1866. He
was known and loved throughout the city and in Frederick
County, Virginia.

After he retired, Dr. Graham was made pastor emeritus
and continued to dwell in Winchester until his death. In
1876 he was honored with a Doctor of Divinity degree
from Hampden-Sydney College. In 1873, he was the
moderator of the Synod of Virginia "and was stated clerk of

The manse in Winchester, Jackson's winter home, 1862.

the Presbytery of Winchester from 1853-1903." Dr. Graham was also moderator of the General Assembly of the Presbyterian Church of the United States, meeting in Nashville in 1894.

He contributed to many religious periodicals, but is best known for "The Planting of the Presbyterian Church in Northern Virginia."

Dr. Graham died on April 8, 1914, in Winchester. He was ninety years old. He was buried in Mount Hebron Cemetery.

The Kent Street Church in Winchester. Courtesy the
Frederick County Historical Society

V

ROBERT LEWIS DABNEY

This preacher who was Jackson's chief of staff was born on March 5, 1820. His birthplace was "at his father's mill place, on the South Anna River, in Louisa County, Virginia." While he was quite young, the family moved to Cub Creek, sixteen miles east of Louisa Court House, and about fifty miles from Richmond. This home three miles south of the road leading to Richmond was very nice. There was a "fine terraced garden, . . . fine old trees, . . . all kinds of shrubbery," an orchard, a garden, stables and barns.[1]

At the age of sixteen, Robert left home to enter Hampden-Sydney. At the end of the first year, he quit to help support his mother. This he did by working in a quarry and by teaching. When things improved, Robert resumed his studies and this time he entered the University of Virginia. He was a student in Charlottesville from 1839 to 1842. During this period he became good friends with a man we have already met, Dr. William S. White. He also became interested in politics and in the slavery question.

Robert made the decision to enter the ministry. However, as we shall see, he took some time between college and seminary. From his graduation in 1842 until October 1844, he managed the family farm and taught school.

November 1844 brought the fulfillment of his hopes and dreams. That autumn month he entered Union Theological Seminary at Hampden-Sydney. Like most ministerial students, he struggled to express himself in speaking and in writing.

When he graduated, Robert became a home missionary

in Louisa County. Then came his first pastorate at Tinkling Springs. He served the parish from July 1847 until August 1853. And during this period, Robert took a wife.

In late summer of 1853, Dabney returned to Hampden-Sydney. This time as professor of Ecclesiastical History and Polity. This was a tremendous opportunity and challenge for a man just thirty-three years old.

It is thought that the original Dabneys were French Huguenots. They spelled their name in many different ways. The family apparently fled to England. From there Robert's ancestors traveled from Norfolk, England, to the banks of the York River.[2]

Charles W., the father of Robert Lewis, married Elizabeth Price in 1808. They resided at the mill place on the South Anna River in Louisa County. There were two mills, a sawmill on one side of the river, and a flour and corn mill on the other side. From there the family moved to Cub Creek in Hanover County.

Charles inherited much of the wealth of his Uncle Charles. Robert and everyone felt that Charles W. was one of the finest men in the area, and most deserving of the inheritance. He was a delegate to the General Assembly of the Presbyterian Church which met in Philadelphia. Along with the religious matters, he was most interested in the city water supply by means of pipes.

Robert's father was taken violently ill with a fever in August of 1833, and died on the sixth of September. He was just forty-nine years old. He left a substantial inheritance for Robert.[3] The family was very close-knit, full of kindness and hospitality. Robert grew up in a "society dominated by plain, homespun gentry."[4] He learned the ways of old Virginia. He listened intently to his father speak of politics. The family was moderately well off, but quite frugal.

Mrs. Dabney was Robert's first teacher. Then he went to a log school taught by his older brother, Charles William.

When the family moved to Cub Creek, there were other teachers. The sons of the planters in Virginia in that day were taught, having "always good teachers and plenty of

91

birch – the teachers being very strict about our manners."[5] Robert enjoyed the spelling bees. As a boy he studied some books that would make a college course look easy. In 1835, Robert rode seven miles on a colt to study for the day under a private teacher.

Robert entered Hampden-Sydney College on June 1, 1836. He was just over sixteen years of age, tall and slender. He was determined to be a scholar, and put forth great effort. He was a good listener, and good at taking notes. Moses D. Hoge was also a student at this Presbyterian school.

Dabney excelled, making the highest marks, and was well prepared to leave and teach himself. He behaved himself well. Even back then there were student problems. Some of the lads rebelled against the college's ban on gambling and organized a protest. The offenders were rounded up, taken into the chapel, and there in the presence of the rest of the student body, "they took a solemn promise to behave well thereafter."[6]

He seems to have realized the value of money and was very careful with his expenditures. He kept himself and his dormitory room very neat. His letters home were very descriptive of the faculty. And between himself and Moses Drury Hoge there was formed "at this time a friendship that was to grow strong and endure every strain till Dr. Hoge should help to bury him, . . . at Hampden-Sydney, in the year 1898."[7]

A letter to his sister Mary would never be selected for the college catalog. Writing of the school he says:

> This place is not very remarkable for anything at all except poverty, for the College stands in the middle of an old field full of gullies and weeds, and the cows of the neighborhood come up to the very windows with their bells, making such a noise that I cannot study. . . . The college is a brick building, four stories high.[8]

He liked the college, yet he found it a dreary place. And there were family matters to think about. His widowed mother was in debt, and faced with the necessity of rebuilding the mill. Robert did not want to be an extra burden, and he felt he could help in the construction project.

The president of the school wrote a letter saying how sorry he was to see Robert leave. At the time, Mrs. Dabney's son was given "the most distinguished rank in scholarship, . . . in behavior, . . . and industry." He was the only one in his class considered "a distinguished scholar."

Just before he left school in the fall of 1837, there was a revival on campus. Robert thought a great deal "about my sins and my eternal salvation." And he made a profession of faith. When he returned home he took communion from his mother's pastor. And forever after, "it remained a *memmorable* day in [my] life."[9]

The rest of 1837 was spent in the stone quarry, and on a boat, hauling stone to rebuild the mill. It was hard work. Then in January of 1838 he opened a neighborhood school. He was still almost two months short of being eighteen himself. He helped build the cabin for the school himself. There were seventeen pupils, and Robert made almost three hundred dollars. In the summer he farmed and when autumn came, he started to teach at another school, walking four miles each way to get there.

In the summer of 1859, Robert went to visit his aunt, Mrs. Rueben Lewis, who lived near Charlottesville. Until this time Robert had considered returning to Hampden-Sydney. But during this visit he became entranced with the University of Virginia. It had a great reputation, and was known as one of the best schools in the South. Graduation from the school established by Thomas Jefferson was a ticket to success.

"His uncle and aunt insisted that he come and live with them; they offered to give him board and lodging for himself and his horse, and urged that he could ride thence to the university and back, . . . and thus complete his education. . . ."[10] It did not take young Robert long to make up his mind. This was an offer too good to pass up.

Robert had to overcome the objections of his friends. In August and again in September, Moses Hoge wrote saying he hoped Robert would return so they could be classmates again. The widow of the renowned Dr. John H. Rice of the faculty wrote him several letters, urging him to return to

Hampden-Sydney, and stating that she felt this was his Christian duty. Another letter said, "I wish I were in a situation to make an offer that might exceed your good aunt's."[11] Hoge and Dabney were looked up to as the most promising students. Therefore, they all hated to lose Robert to the liberal University of Virginia.

December 9, 1839, to July 5, 1842, were the years Dabney spent at the University of Virginia. The university, like the little college, was hit with ferment and change. It must have been like the 1960s of our day, only with less violence.

Robert, in January of 1840, writes:

> It is quite a pretty place, though I suspect I do not think it quite as pretty as Mr. Jefferson used to think it. . . . They have a library of 16,000 volumes, and a collection of some thousands of paintings and engravings.[12]

These however, did no one any good. There was no place to display them. He felt his teachers were quite adequate, and again described them in his letters home. He also took a swipe at the sons of the rich who were spoiled and undisciplined. Some of them would not wear a coat for more than two months.[13] "These are the chaps to spend $1,500 or $2,000, and learn about three cents worth of useful learning and enough rascality to ruin them forever. . . . Students are the most inflammable beings that ever existed, and they must be managed with the greatest promptness and skill, for when they once get away, they are unmanageable." Robert was really concerned about the lack of principles, and the wild oats carrying over into the adult years.[14]

Apparently the students were noted for their disorderly behavior. Jefferson expected them to act like adults, and they did not. Professors could not control the classes, and many resigned. During Dabney's second year, a Professor Davis of the Law School was murdered. This occurred during a student riot. Dr. White also lamented the behavior of the students at the University of Virginia.

Dabney was also shocked at the dress code of the

women. He had his own high standards from rural Virginia. He thought fancy shoes and bright clothes, especially for older women, were out of order.

Robert devoted his energies to study and mastered Latin, Greek, French, and Italian, and worked on the library papers. He also joined the Jefferson Society. He wrote letters to the editor of the *Charlottesville Jeffersonian*. These had fine literary merit. Robert also entered into a Bible study class. He pledged himself to "total abstinence." There were thirty young men in the temperance society. Dabney felt that if they could keep one young man from becoming addicted to the evils of strong drink, it would be worthwhile.

During these days, Dabney became friends with Dr. William S. White. He served the Presbyterian Church in the area where Dabney's aunt and uncle lived. Writing to his mother on January 4, 1840, Robert said:

> He [White] is a very friendly man, and offered me the use of his books and invited me to his house. I am very much pleased with him. I have not heard him preach yet. . . .[15]

He wrote again in October of Dr. White, saying that he was gaining in stature all the time. "There are few men in the State who does more good than he does. . . . His church is flourishing. . . ." Dabney stopped often to chat with White, and to listen to his wisdom. "Thus began and grew the friendship cherished by each to the end of life."

Maintaining his political interests, Dabney was a confirmed Democrat. He took time to attend the speeches given by Virginia and national leaders in Charlottesville.

He was also refining his views on slavery, of which "there was no greater curse." He had no time for the abolitionists either. Before they began to meddle in Virginia affairs, there was a good possibility that slavery would have been ended in Virginia within twenty years. The abolitionist movement in Dabney's eyes,[16] "has almost broken the ties of political union, and thrown back the poor slave from his hope of approaching emancipation. At least half a century, which, in short, has been to our view productive of nothing but evil. . . ."[17]

Dabney was charitable to those who treated the slaves kindly, but felt something should be done to those who abused them. He did not like the court system which handed down a light sentence to a white man arrested for a crime, but gave severe punishment to a black man for the same offense.

Dabney was interested in many things: other letters home to his brothers, talk about the management of the farm, planting and rotation of crops, and fertilizing the fields.

In the meantime, brother Francis was thinking about going to VMI. Robert wrote to his younger sister, using four pages urging her not to put off her decision for Christ. He told her the longer she resisted, the harder it would be to say "yes" to the Master.

Hoge was impressed with Dabney's penmanship, "It seems to me that your pen is always rampant—curling its very feathers with impatience to entertain some far-away acquaintance." Dabney's biographer says, "The fountain of energy in him ran a bold stream, and the waters divided and ran in many fructifying channels."[18]

Robert paid for his education by earning six hundred dollars teaching. He sold a horse for one hundred fifty dollars, and borrowed another one hundred fifty from his uncle. His expenses for his senior year at VMI amounted to four hundred dollars. Today students would balk at riding a horse over five miles a day to school, much of the time in the cold, and over muddy roads. Robert felt the cold weather improved his health.

Robert graduated in 1842, then followed another two-year interval. He had considered the ministry before going to Charlottesville. But it seems he needed a little more time to think about it. He did not announce his intentions because he did not want to be treated differently at the university. He maintained a prudent silence. Moses Hoge and his aunt and uncle felt he should enter seminary immediately, but others in the family needed money to attend school.

So it seems that the delay was for added time to think,

and also to ease the financial burden for his mother. Robert returned home to manage the farm, and to accumulate some funds for seminary. He helped to pay for his sister Betty's education, sent his brother off to VMI, and opened a classical school in the family home. From this he earned four hundred dollars. He wrote an entire Latin grammar for his sister Betty.

"He was a man capable of success in any one of many fields." Thomas Ritchie, editor of the *Richmond Inquirer*, and a leading Democrat, offered him a salary of twelve hundred dollars a year, and a percentage of the profits, to edit the party publications in Petersburg. Another friend said, "Nature meant you for an editor. . . . There is no man in the Union your superior as a writer."[19] Perhaps this is why Dabney was able to do such a fine job so quickly on his later book about Jackson. The following summer he was offered the job as a classical teacher in Richmond.

These were all turned down, and in the fall of 1844 he entered Union Seminary, located at the time at Hampden-Sydney. It was a small school, three professors and eighteen students. He had a rough time getting there. Robert went to Richmond and took a canal boat to Cartersville. The captain was drunk and got into a fight with an Irish passenger who was also drunk. The last leg of the journey was via stage.[20]

He obtained a nice room in the main building of the seminary. And the boardinghouse served good meals. There was little social life, but on December 4, 1845, he went to a "candy stew" at the home of Professor Graham's. Everything in the house was old-fashioned, and done just like things were done in the country.

Robert finished three years' work in two years. At the same time he copied a manuscript for publication, wrote articles for publication, preached quite a few sermons, read "widely, visited a good deal, made some excursions, and spent his surplus energy in corresponding."[21] His was the kind of energy that Jackson could appreciate. There was no time for idleness.

On July 8, 1845, Robert preached his first sermon in one

97

of Dr. Graham's little country churches. The crowd was critical. Two leaned on their elbows, but none fell asleep, on the hot Sunday. Robert wrote, "I found preaching tired me, both body and voice, much more than I expected." He was convinced from his first experience, that he could never read sermons to his people. They had to come from the heart.

He wrote about missions and philosophical ideas. His thesis for graduation was "What Causes Checked the Progress of the Reformation?" Titles and messages were long in those days. He sold a magazine article "A Series of Articles on the Second Commandment and Popish Idolatry."

Illness hit him in 1846, a liver ailment, and trouble with weak eyes. At first he was afraid he was going to lose his sight. He believed very much in exercise. He found this by chopping the wood for his room, by taking care of his own watermelon patch, building a summer house on the campus and doing other things to beautify the campus. He had seventy-five hills of watermelons.

Once he rode to Farmville and was very much impressed with a factory full of blacks singing hymns. "They sing with very great effect, and fully maintained their reputation as musical geniuses. Indeed, some of the finest vocal music I ever heard was in this factory. They carry three or four parts. He felt the masters of slaves should encourage the music, and that the Presbyterian Church should consider the music of the blacks in regards to setting the Psalms to music.

After graduation, Robert headed for Louisa County. His mother was a widow, and lonely. One day she looked at her son's room, and said, "[It] looks like there has been a death in it. Indeed, I know not what I shall do without you." Despite his youth, the family seemed to turn to Robert for strength and comfort. A ministry in the county would permit him to stay with his mother, and at the same time, reach out to the poverty-stricken folks in the county.

At first, Robert was leery of accepting the work. After all, "A prophet is without honor in his own country." Most of the folks knew him, and many were related to him. However, an elder in the Providence Church wrote, "As the son of a man to whom the people of Lousia, and all, . . . who knew him, delighted to do honor, you will stand on higher ground that any stranger could."[22] Elder Minor told him not to expect an easy road. "The minister's life is truly a life of crosses. . . . He must expect to have his sermons found fault with." Sometimes the messages would be too plain, sometimes too profound. Some would expect them to be read, others not even written out. Elder Minor urged the young man to pray.

Robert accepted the circuit. It took him about a month to get around to each preaching place. The people were impressed with his compassion and complete dependence on the Lord. The last item was another point common to the life of Jackson. And the folks were deeply impressed with his sermons.

He was licensed to preach in May of 1846. The Providence Church, and "the South Anna and Green Springs neighborhoods in Louisa county"[23] became his parish as a home mission field.

The work was of short duration. He had suffered from colic, and there seems to have been some malaria in the area. His doctor felt he would never be cured by medicine, "Your hope is in a change of climate and water. You must get into a region entirely free from malaria, and drink limestone water."[24] Dr. William Meredith also notes that no one ever had a chill in Staunton.

Ten days later, Dabney got a serious overture from "the Tinkling Springs Church, of Augusta County, seven miles from Staunton." Dabney must have thought about the physician's remark and Providence. He went to visit Tinkling Springs, stayed two weeks, and had no health problems.

He received a letter dated April 19, 1847, saying that he had been elected pastor of the Tinkling Springs Church. There were only two dissenting votes. The committee said the geographical area was good, there were many young families, and the church had been without a pastor for eighteen months. He had labored for a year in Louisa

County for three hundred dollars. The new congregation was offering to double the salary.

Sadly, Robert got off on the wrong foot. His colic acted up on his first Sunday, causing him to miss his initial appearance as pastor, "There was a tremendous congregation, and all agog with curiosity to see my debut." This was the beginning of six years and two months of service. The people were Scotch-Irish. At times they were "very inflexible and obstinate." He felt they were obstinate when right, and mulish when wrong, and this played right into the hands of the devil. He lamented the petty acts which are seen so often in building and other church programs. However, the church is not a rest home for the saints, but a hospital for imperfect sinners. In January of 1849 he suffered great depression over the absence of spiritual life and commitment in the church.

But things went forward and a new church was built. This despite disagreements over the bricks in the building. He wrote to Dr. White in Lexington about his feelings, and was comforted by words of encouragement from the man who was to become Jackson's pastor. White said the truth of Jesus Christ was the answer. "Preach as if your preaching was everything, and then pray as if it were nothing."[25]

The church did not have a manse. So at first Robert stayed with Hugh Guthrie. A lifelong fellowship developed. Dabney stayed here until the end of 1849.

In the meantime, in August of 1847, the Presbytery was to convene at Bethesda Church. Rev. James Morrison, of New Providence, Rockbridge County, invited Robert to stop at his place en route. This was at Bellevue. Robert accepted the invitation. He was met by Mr. Morrison who reminded the young cleric of Robert E. Lee.

Robert had been told by his colleagues that the Reverend Mr. Morrison had a very sweet daughter by the name of Lavina. So he may have had ulterior motives. She was about twenty-four years of age at the time. Robert did not meet her until the next day. He was immediately smitten by her looks and personality. The following day they went for a horseback ride. "She was a very fine rider, and could manage her horse perfectly. I thought she was remarkably graceful. Mine was very nearly a case of 'love at first sight.' . . . Then began the first and last love affair of my life. We were married on the twenty-eighth of March 1848."[26] Dabney got the wife "appointed him by Providence."

The young couple lived with Mr. Guthrie for a time. Dabney loved the land and farming. Thus, he started to look around for a piece of ground where he could have a home of his own. Inflation was a problem way back then. The reason, the railroad was being built to White Sulphur Springs, making the market high.

But he managed to scrape the money together, and on October 3, 1849, purchased "Sleepy Hollow, a little homestead on the main road between Staunton and Waynesboro, quite convenient to the church. . . . It is a poor place, but the only habitable one . . . in which I could hide my head at all at the present time. It contains about one acre of timber and nine acres of open land." There was a good well, the cottage contained four rooms, a small stable, and an outhouse in poor condition. The cost was nine hundred dollars with half of the payment due at time of sale. He felt this would provide not only a home but a good investment. There was a great influx of Germans at the time, and they "are always land-mad."[27]

Dabney did quite well, living here for three years, and having added assets of two horses and two cows. He was able to hire a black man to help with the chores and cook. All of this on six hundred dollars a year. This salary enabled him to live "happy as a king," and at the same time entertain a lot.

Dabney prospered and sold "Sleepy Hollow" for thirteen hundred dollars. With the money, he purchased 120 acres nearby. He called this purchase, "Stony Point." Here he built a stone house, doing most of the work himself. He and his wife moved in on January 1, 1853.

Dabney seems to have been a jack of all trades. He could have been a success in almost any literary field. He had been an excellent student, and was looked upon as a fine teacher and preacher. He was also very skilled with his hands, making excellent furniture and other wood designed products. And we have seen that he could do masonary work. Robert was also an outstanding farmer and orchardist. In working for his mother, and on his own place, he used methods and ideas, far ahead of his own time. It seems that he was never idle. He was constantly writing articles for publication in newspapers, and in religious and academic journals.

Some of these articles were about slavery. The institution affected every phase of life in the 1800s. The churches, North and South, were also torn apart by the issue. Generally speaking, all the *preachers Jackson knew,* felt as he did about the issue. They were opposed to system. It was not right for one man to own another, and it was definitely wrong for a black family to be split up by the sale of the husband or wife. Dabney and White spoke and wrote on the issue. Their papers constitute a story of their own.

Meanwhile, Union Seminary was declining. It had little to offer. Dr. Graham died, leaving two professors and eleven students. The brightest and best of young Virginia Presbyterians went to Princeton or Columbia. Dabney often wrote in Presbyterian journals that this problem should be corrected. He said that the Lord and the Synod were sad over the state of affairs. The seminary should be built up and young Virginians encouraged to attend.

Sometimes when we are critical of a situation, we are called upon to be a part of the answer. Looked upon as a bright and talented young man, the trustees elected Robert L. Dabney to become part of the staff at Union Seminary at Hampden-Sydney.

Moses D. Hoge felt that Robert was the ideal man to bring new life to Union. Yet it was hard for Robert to pull up stakes and leave Tinkling Springs. When the spring of 1853 rolled around, he was happy in his ministry in rural Virginia. Not only was he preaching, and doing his pastoral work, but he had begun a classical school. He was building a home, farming, and doing a lot of writing.

One Saturday, he was out in his corn patch doing some

planting with a hired Negro. Mrs. Dabney sent a boy to call him, saying, "Mrs. Dabney says come to the house. Who do you suppose has been elected professor in Union Theological Seminary?" "Who?" "She says you are." So that's how he got the news. If he accepted, a great many changes would have to be made. He was loathe to leave the comfort of his new home, and wondered what effect Prince Edward County would have on his health.

His friend, Dr. William S. White, wrote, "I regard the position to which you are invited as more important than any pastoral charge in the land. . . . Your habits, tastes, and general qualifications fit you for the station. . . . This office will furnish you, through God's blessing, not only to serve your own, but succeeding generations. . . . Your place at Tinkling Spring may readily be supplied—that at the Seminary cannot be. My heart's desire and prayer to God is, that you may see the finger of God pointing directly to acceptance."[28] To White's letters were added scores of others, urging Dabney to accept.

At the age of thirty-three, Dabney was honored with a Doctor of Divinity Degree. And he made the choice to return to Hampden-Sydney and Union as professor of Ecclesiastical History and Polity. The longest journey begins with the first step. Robert L. Dabney made the choice or the step in 1853 that would link him for thirty years with Union Seminary. During that period, he held two professorships, and was co-pastor of the College Church.

Seminary Professor

Once he arrived at Seminary and commenced his work, Robert threw himself into his task. He wrote later to a friend, "Nobody can doubt that to train up many pastors, and thus multiply yourself is better than to do the work of one pastor." That seems to have been his objective. To all his students, he stressed reading, research, and meditation. He warned them "that if they were lazy as students, they would be lazy as future ministers."[29]

Robert had great energy. He traveled during vacation at his own expense to raise endowment money. And he visited many churches, colleges, and universities stressing the benefits of Union and acting as a good public relations man. In the summer of 1858 he made a trip to North Carolina, and then another one throughout Virginia. During the latter trip he spoke at Tinkling Springs, Lexington, Winchester, Martinsburg, Berkeley Springs, Falling Waters, Moorefield, Charles Town, Cumberland (Maryland), and several other places.[30]

In 1856 he was made chairman of the building committee. He designed the building of another house, and superintended the construction of it. Two years later he was asked to help with the senior class in the field of Systematic and Polemic Theology. Things were looking up. New professors came, and the student body increased to thirty-eight students. At Dabney's instigation, the course of study was revised. The Bible was made the center of studies, and the Biblical Department, the most important of the seminary. He was offered the presidency of the seminary in 1858, but declined.

Thus the late fifties were spent in teaching, and traveling in behalf of the seminary. Dabney also found time to write a *Memoir of Dr. Sampson,* one of the founders of Union. This went into four printings. The synod also desired the publication of a magazine carrying conservative theological, moral, evangelical, and ethical views in harmony with the Presbyterian Church. Dabney and Hoge took the lead in getting the *Central Presbyterian* off the ground.

Sectional differences were still on the horizon, and the slavery issue was simmering. "The Clay Compromise" had quieted things down and postponed the inevitable. Dabney wrote an article "Pray for Your Country." It would be good to use it today. He said that the storm was coming, the politicians were powerless to avert it. Dabney said the "country would be ruined unless God interposed, and the Christian conscience came to the rescue. It reads like prophecy."[31] "Pray for Your Country" came out in the *Central Presbyterian,* and then in several other church publications.

In 1857, the president of Hampden-Sydney College went

to Kentucky. The trustees asked Dabney to teach a course in Mental and Moral Philosophy. This was for the senior class. He agreed and was paid $320. All were impressed with his teaching, and he was then elected president of the college.

The previous year he had gone to the General Assembly of the denomination. He wrote home describing New York, and in 1858 he was chosen to preach to the meeting of the Board of Foreign Missions. Even though he was located at a small school in the hills of Virginia, Dabney was gaining a great reputation and was in great demand.

In letters to the family and close friends, Dabney shared his fears about the coming storm. He felt, as many still feel, that the politicians were up to mischief. He urged moderation and caution not only in the South but in the North as well. He expounded on the duty of "Christian people to save the country from coming political evils."[32] Sounds like the Moral Majority of today.

But war was coming. In the autumn of 1859 the seminary had grown to thirty-six students. Twenty-five of these were from the Synod of Virginia. Endowment had grown from $58,000 to $90,000. Those connected with the seminary felt "all this growth was due to Robert L. Dabney more than to all others put together." During this time, Dabney also served as pastor of the College Church. Young and old alike were fascinated by his descriptive preaching and eloquence. Many in the denomination wanted him to go to Princeton. He was offered a post there. In response, he wrote a letter several pages long, stating that although he appreciated the honor, he felt his place was at Union.

A friend, urging Dabney to stay at Union, wrote:

> The fate of Presbyterianism in Virginia is bound up in that Seminary, the one falls with the other. Your removal will kill the Seminary, . . . and with it Presbyterians in Virginia.[33]

Then came the John Brown Raid, and in 1860 the election of Abraham Lincoln. Virginia Christians were very much disturbed. One of the reasons Dabney turned down the offer to go to Princeton was the belief that the abolitionists would force the country into war before he had a chance to get a fair start. And he would not side "with the fanatics and usurpers against his own state and people."

Many expressed surprise at Dabney's feelings and prophecy of war. But he saw it coming. As stated earlier, he felt ministers and Christians should do everything they could to stop it. In "Christians, Pray for Your Country," Dabney had said:

> National passions of the Free Soil party were clothing themselves in the garb of religion and becoming as ungovernable as a storm, and as implacable as death. Already, do the low mutterings of the rising cloud of civil war come from our Western borders. Let that cloud break forth into the thunder of battle, and before the winds have swept its roar to the Atlantic, the angry passions now smouldering in magazine will be lit into universal blaze, as if by the touch of lightning. Let those weapons, now pointed against each other in angry array, be once lifted up to the nation, reeking from fratricidal slaughter, and they will muster the foeman from the North and South to the battle. . . .

Dabney foresaw the election of Lincoln, and thought that he would bring the government to bear to disgrace and oppress the South, while the Gulf States would act too rashly, and open the conflict. He was close to being correct.

On the Sunday after Lincoln's election, he preached a stirring sermon, urging the people to remain cool, and pray for peace. He called for them to carry their Christian faith into every aspect of their lives. He called for them to turn a deaf ear and the other cheek to those from the North who had misrepresented and painted a false picture of the South. "Every Christian must study the things that make for peace."[34]

Sadly, some took parts of the sermon, quoted it out of context, and looked upon it as encouraging aggression. By the twenty-eighth of December, Dabney writes, "I feel sick at heart at the state of our country. I have been attempting, in my feeble way, to preach peace, and to rouse Christians to their duty in staying the tide of passion and violence."

Some of his friends in the North were trying to get the ear of moderate congressman and senators. Some felt that arresting the abolitionist aggression might help. Yet even the Christians had seemingly lost "their senses with excitement, fear, and passion and everything seems to be hurrying to civil war. . . . Three-fourths of the people there [North] are for peace; but we seem to be given up of God, and the violent ones have it all their own way. As for South Carolina, the little impudent vixen has gone beyond all patience. She is as great a pest as the Abolitionists."

In January, Dabney wrote another appeal to the clergy and Christians of the nation. Once again he called for "moderation, calmness and Christian patience, on the part of both sections . . . [in] the tempest of excitement [shaking] the nation."

Dabney discussed the sacred shrines of the country, the united efforts against Europe, and said a conflict would destroy our personal security and standing in the world, and would disgrace our system of government. He also talked about the hardship war would bring to the church and to missionary endeavors. The step into war should be deferred as long as "there is a spark of hope. . . . That final step is so solemn and may be so awful, should not every honorable means for avoiding it necessarily be exhausted by the good man before he takes it. . . .?"

> Let us, then, all study moderation of political sentiment, of resentment and of language. Let us keep a watch before the door of our lips.

He called for the use of the Sabbath to speak peace and to pray for peace.

In considering the consequences of a rash act, Dabney asked his hearers to bring before their minds the picture of "a country ravaged; its fields, . . . stained by battle; . . . its cities sacked or deserted; its peaceful homes desolated, . . . and let him ask himself whether, as he stands amidst the ruins, he will be able to take heaven to witness that none of the guilt is in his skirts."

Dabney called them all to remember that they would have to answer at the judgment seat of Christ about their conduct as citizens, and to keep in mind that their actions would contribute to the agony of the widows, the orphans, and gray-haired parents. He called for new commitment to God, feeling that although the situation was bad, "all is not yet lost."

Many leading Virginians signed their name to the appeal. Over in Lexington, on the fourteenth of January others read the appeal of the sermon. And under these words:

> We, the undersigned, cordially concur in the general tone of sentiment and feeling expressed in the foregoing paper:
> Rev. William N. Pendleton, D.D., Rector of Grace Church, Episcopal.
> Rev. William S. White, D.D., Presbyterian Church.
> Rev. George Junkin, D.D.
> John T. L. Preston, Virginia Military Institute.
> T. J. Jackson, Professor, Virginia Military Institute.[35]

Until the very last, Dabney did not regard Lincoln's election as a cause for secession. He regarded the conduct of South Carolina as unjustifiable. He felt the state had made "a wanton breach of Federal compacts, and disregard of vested rights." Yet South Carolina had taken a stand that would probably cause the rest of the South to stand or fall with her.

Dabney writes:

> We should remember that America is one in race, in geography, in language, in material interests. Even if we angrily divide, there will be powerful interests drawing us together again, after the wire edge of our spite is worn off. Every good man, ever after separation seems inevitable, should try to act with a view to the speediest reunion.

Once again, he seems to have been a real prophet.

The moderates were not to prevail. War came, and with it hardship and suffering, both physical and emotional for Dabney and thousands of others.

January 1862 found Dabney trying to enter the army as a chaplain in Cabell's artillery. Jackson saw the letter and wrote that Mr. Lacy had been at his headquarters, but had gone to Orange Court House to minister in the hospitals. The general was sorry but he had no openings on his staff at the moment.

However, in March, Anna Jackson, in the face of the Union advance, left Winchester. She came to Hampden-

Robert Lewis Dabney. Courtesy the
Presbyterian Historical Foundation

Sydney and took refuge with Dr. Dabney. She wrote to her
husband about the energetic preacher.[36]

From Mount Jackson, the general wrote to Dabney on
March 29, 1862, saying if he entered the army, he hoped
he would come to the Valley District. If that did not work
out, and he could get a commission, "and would be willing
to take a position on my staff as an aide-de-camp, I will try
and secure it for you, with the understanding that you will
remain with me until the war terminates." Jackson con-

Moses Drury Hoge. Courtesy the Presbyterian Historical Foundation

cluded his letter by saying, "I am thankful to God for sending so many of his children into this army, and my prayer is, that he will continue to send them. . . ."

Jackson had already received a letter from Dabney about the possibility of partisan warfare. The general deemed that impractical at the moment. The preacher also thought like Jackson. "Had Dr. Dabney been the President of the Confederacy, . . . he would have made Titanic exertions to push it with effective, sweeping vigor," including an invasion of the North.

Ten days later the post of adjutant general became vacant. And Jackson wrote to Dabney, telling him to take the recommendation, "go to Richmond, get the appointment and join me at once; provided you can make your arrangements to remain with me for the remainder of the war. Your rank will be that of major. Your duties will require early rising and industry."[37]

Jackson expected commitment. He repeated again his wishes that Dabney sign up for the duration. Mrs. Jackson urged Dabney to accept her husband's invitation. Robert consulted Dr. Atkinson, president of the college. About the middle of April he rode to see Jackson at Swift Run Gap. "He went without horse, uniform or arms. His chief 'purpose was to show to General Jackson how unfit' he was for the post offered." Robert thought perhaps a chaplaincy would be better. The general overruled all the objections, and gave Dabney two days to read Halleck's "Articles of War." Then the Presbyterian preacher was installed as a member of Jackson's staff.

Robert wrote to his mother saying that she would be as surprised to hear from him as he was surprised at being with Jackson. Her son told her that the seminary was to be closed due to the war, and he did not want to be idle. He thought he had better accept a good offer when it was given.

He writes again on May 6:

> The adjutant is pretty much the General's secretary; . . . I always eat at the same table, and most frequently sleep in the same room. . . . He treats me with the greatest kindness and consideration; . . . he is exact and exacting in an official point of view to all under him, personally he is almost embarrassingly kind. . . .

On Sunday, May 18, Dabney conducted services near Mount Solon. In attendance were Jackson and Richard S. Ewell. Old Baldy was very much concerned about the military situation. However, he was greatly comforted by Dabney's sermon "Come unto me, all ye that labor and are heavy laden, and I will give you rest."

Dabney preached a month later at the camp of Winder's brigade. In the afternoon, communion was served in the camp in the woods. Even Jed Hotchkiss felt Dabney gave a fine sermon. Jackson was there, drinking in every word, sitting "humbly devout."[38]

Colonel Grigsby of the Stonewall brigade was a rather profane man. Soon after Dabney arrived on the scene, the colonel went to Jackson's quarters. Returning to his own tent he was asked, "What about the new Adjutant?" Grigsby replied:

> I concluded that old Jack must be a fatalist sure enough, when he put in an Ironside Presbyterian parson, as his chief of staff, but I have bright hopes of headquarters, seeing they are no longer omniscient.[39]

Grigsby told it like he saw it when he said later, of Dabney, "Our parson is not afraid of Yankee bullets, and I tell you he preaches like hell." Apparently Robert did find the time to preach often, and he also visited the sick and wounded soldiers.

Dabney wrote detailed letters of the various actions to his family. These later helped him to write his book on Jackson. At first Dabney thought that Jackson pushed his men too hard. "His victories are as fatal to his own armies as to his enemies. The former he kills, the latter he works nearly to death."[40] As time went by, he understood Jackson's methods and art of conducting warfare.

At Port Republic on Sunday, June 8, 1862, Dabney was given credit for saving Jackson's trains.

Before Jackson left for Charlottesville, he had to give someone an idea of what was happening. He took Dabney into his confidence. Calling the clergyman to a hotel room, he locked the door, and then whispered his plan. Jackson was going ahead of the army. He had to head for Richmond to confer with Lee. The army was to head east, and rejoin the main force at Richmond. Jackson would be back to rejoin them, probably near Fredericks Hall. "In the meantime, Dabney would be in charge of the march along the Virginia Central right of way. Secrecy had to be insured."[41]

Dabney had to deal with Ewell's anger over not being

told about the movement, and also over Harman's rumors which were very upsetting. Ewell thought the major had been told more than he.

Military duty, Jackson's demands, and the swamps along the Chickahominy all took their toll on Dabney. He became ill and resigned.

Jackson told Samuel Morrison:

> Major Dabney wishes to resign on account of his health; I hope that after a while he can remain in the field.

Exhaustion had rendered Dabney unfit for duty. Jackson, naturally, had to approve the resignation, "but he did it with the greatest reluctance, . . . [considering Dabney] the most efficient officer he knew." Jackson had been pleased with the clergyman's performance, and at the moment knew of no one to take his place.[42]

The resignation was accepted with reluctance in September. Thus, his brief military career was over. Col. G. F. R. Henderson, in writing on failures at Cedar Run in midsummer states, "The absence of Major Dabney, struck down by sickness, is a possible explanation of faulty orders."

Dabney's recovery was very slow. While he was still ill, three of his children were struck down by diphtheria. Thomas Price, perhaps the brightest of the Dabney children, died.

Robert then went back to the seminary. There were only four students. Inflation was hitting hard. Hogs sold for $30.00 a hundred, and corn at $8.60 a barrel.

Dabney was a devoted Confederate. And even while ill, he came up with the idea of fighting for his beloved South with his pen. So he wrote a little book, *The Defense of Virginia and the South.* His object was to refute the slanders of the North against the institutions of the South. He felt that the South needed a good image at home and abroad. Government leaders looked at his work and were very much impressed. They decided to have it published in London and circulated in Europe. However, one of the Confederate commissioners there objected to one of the points, and disobeyed the Richmond government, refusing to have it printed. After the war, some Southern leaders expressed the opinion that Dabney's book would have been excellent public relations material, and might have enlisted European aid.

From the Fredericksburg area, Dabney received a letter dated December 5:

> . . . I much regret that your health would not permit you to remain longer in service with the army in the field, but I am very thankful to God for having permitted me to have the privilege of being blessed with your Christian and military labors as long as he did; and my hope is that your health is improving, and that it will soon be what it was before you joined me. Whilst we were near Winchester, it pleased our ever merciful Heavenly Father to visit my command with the rich outpouring of his spirit. There were probably more than a hundred inquiring the way of life in my old brigade. It appears to me that we may look for growing piety and many conversions in the army.
>
> T. J. Jackson[43]

This was the revival at Bunker Hill, led by Dr. Stiles and others.

Jackson wrote another letter to Dabney from Moss Neck on January 1, 1863. He was grateful for the prayer meetings Dr. White and Dabney were having and for prayer for the army. "I have more confidence in such organizations than of military ones being the means of leading to an early peace. . . ."[44]

Things were getting increasingly worse for the people of Virginia. Family letters talked of the Yankees taking and shooting fine horses, chickens, and hogs. They even took the mules of the blacks.

Dabney then turned his literary endeavors toward telling the story of General Jackson. Sometime after Chancellorsville, he visited Mrs. Jackson in North Carolina, and after Gettysburg, conferred with General Lee. He finished the work just before Appomattox. The biography was first published by Nesbit and Company in London, and again by a New York firm in 1867. Other biographies have appeared. But the one written by the seminary professor and staff officer is still a standard reference.

Robert treats the civil questions between the two sections. He explains Jackson's character and religious life. Colonel Henderson pays another tribute: "I . . . acknowledge the debt I owe to a soldier and writer of such conspicuous ability. Not only have I quoted freely from his pages, but he was good enough, at my request, to write exhaustive memoranda on disputed points."[45]

After Gettysburg, Dabney realized that things were bad for the South. He went to Orange Court House and while watching a review of A. P. Hill's corps, spoke with advisers to General Lee and President Davis, urging great sacrifices on the part of the people of the South.

Dabney felt the Confederate leaders had to realize that victory was hopeless unless there was help from abroad. He felt the South had to be willing to pay for the aid. One method would be by gradual emanicipation. Dabney said that both the governments of the North and South had their hands tied by the "fanatical anti-slavery movement." Lincoln had been smart to issue the Emancipation Proclamation. This was a fine, expedient, political move. He was fearful that when the people reached the point of being willing to sacrifice, it would be too late.

Mrs. Dabney fell ill in the summer of 1864. Robert sent her to a health resort, and kept the home fires burning, "acting the part of an old hen, keeping house, drying fruit, making molasses, etc."

Things were getting dark in the fall of 1864. Robert kept hearing news of young men dying, and also the suffering of the civilians. One of his great efforts led to the uniting of the Synod of the South with the Presbyterian Church in the Confederate States of America. This was a major achievement.

During the winter, there were no students at the seminary, so Dabney served as a missionary to the army. On December 11, he spoke to a large gathering of soldiers at the New Market Methodist Church. The weather forced him to return home. He then opened his home to care for sick and wounded soldiers.

He was also at Petersburg during the last days of the retreat. Robert was with the army at Appomattox, and hid out to escape being sent to a Northern prison. Returning home, he found it had been pillaged.

Robert was crushed by the fall of the Confederacy. He had grown up in Virginia, and loved the old way of life. "To be governed and to know that his beloved country was governed by aliens, was as the bitterness of death." He was fearful of black control and of what Northern leaders might do. "Universal change and unrest were the order of the day."[46] The people were quiet in Virginia, but their irritation and hurt were deep.

For a while, Dabney considered leaving the country, but he remained because of loyalty to his mother, and out of a sense of duty to others. He had served the Confederacy with all his resources, his purse, pen, time, and active duty. Now all that remained was to pick up the pieces. His money was gone. Proceeds from the sale of the farm at Tinkling Springs had gone into Confederate bonds, and his gold watch was sold for the cause. He did own twenty bales of cotton, his carriage horses, and two cows.

Like his neighbors, Dabney was left "without slaves, without money, without fences, with little livestock, little corn and no meat." By 1870, the situation was even worse. Robert wrote to his mother in mid-February of 1868, expressing the idea that he wished he were in her shoes, older, and ready to depart from the world and the painful experiences of Reconstruction. He wondered what was ahead for his poor little children.

Earlier he had stated to Moses Hoge, "I see we are whipped, I regard . . . all . . . as lost." Everything he had staked his life on was gone. He kept thinking about moving to be free of Yankee dominion, but few were ready to join him.

To gain money to leave, he opened a private school for young ladies in his house. Eight boarded in his home, and there were eleven day students. With Mrs. Dabney's help, he saved one thousand dollars in greenbacks.

Just after the war, it looked like the seminary might not reopen. The leadership had invested $46,000 in Confederate bonds. This was all gone. However, Presbyterians in Baltimore and New York came to their aid. Students soon returned. Most of them, like James Smith, wearing Confederate gray. They had to cover their military buttons with black. This was required by occupation rules. Dr. White in Lexington had been one who urged the reopening of the seminary.

There are many pages in the book devoted to this period of Dabney's life. It is interesting reading, and tells of the suffering of those living in that period. However, it does not pertain to Jackson and his relationship with Dabney.

R. L. Dabney was at the height of his powers in the postwar years, and "was the dominant force in the Seminary and a potent voice throughout the Church." He was strongly conservative and sought true spirituality in the church. Again, he and Jackson were alike to this thinking.

In 1883, his health broke, and he resigned to seek a warmer climate. He moved to Texas, on the advice of a doctor. However, other matters entered into his decision. He found it very hard to accept the Confederate defeat, and he felt that the postwar changes left Hampden-Sydney off the main thoroughfare of life.

Dabney still had some of the pioneer spirit. He looked upon life on the frontier in Texas as holding some of the best of what had been found in Old Virginia. He was always able to make friends, especially with "folks of clean lives, high aspirations, and noble endeavor."[47]

He purchased some ground two blocks from the university in Austin and lived there until 1895. He was professor of Moral Philosophy and Political Economy. He combined psychology and theology in his teachings. He wrote a book on philosophy and articles on "Emotions." Naturally, he continued to write for church periodicals. He even tried his hand at poetry.

A Texas lawyer once introduced Dabney as a "teacher, pastor, author, philosopher, logician, historian, patriot, soldier, Christian."[48] This was R. L. Dabney, a preacher Jackson knew.

He developed a bladder disease and went blind. Yet he continued to preach, and gave a most memorable address to the Presbyterian Assembly in 1897. He was led to the speaker's stand.

Knowing the end was near, he prepared a message for his family:

> To My dear Sons and Daughters and their Children:
>
> I desire before I leave the world, as my best legacy to my family, my serious solemn advice, to make choice of God for their God. He has been my father's God, and the God of your Mother's predecessors. I solemnly charge you to make it your first care to seek after peace with God, and being reconciled, to make it your study to please God in all things.
>
> Wait diligently upon the means of grace, attending the worship of God in His house; study His word, after secret prayer and the public ordinances. . . .
>
> Cry to the Lord for communion with him. . . .
>
> Follow God fully, without turning aside. . . .
>
> Be good to your mother, as you would have God's blessing. She will need your comfort.
>
> The sum of the Gospel is Christ crucified. I commit my body to the dust. . . . My spirit I commit to my Lord Jesus Christ; to him I have entrusted it long ago.
>
> Now, my dear boys, this is my last legacy, that we all meet where there is no more death, sorrow nor sin.
>
> > Your devoted father,
> > R. L. Dabney[49]

On Sunday, January 2, 1898, Dabney wished to attend church. The day was cold and raw, so he stayed home. The next morning he dressed, ate breakfast, and dictated a biographical sketch of Dr. Francis Sampson. Late in the evening, he developed a severe chest pain. Dabney knew his time had come. He prayed that he might go quickly. The prayer was answered. At 10:50 p.m., on Monday evening, January 3, he joined Jackson and his own children across the river.

He had told his sons that he wished to be buried in a little cemetery belonging to Union Theological Seminary in Hampden-Sydney. Here he had met his wife and spent so much of his life. Here many of his friends were buried and also three of his little children.

The body was brought by train from Victoria to Farmville. There a delegation of students and teachers from the college and seminary were waiting. They escorted the casket to the College Church. Several speakers shared in the service, including one of Dr. White's sons now serving in Winchester. Moses D. Hoge was the last speaker. Then the folks left the church and made their way to the little cemetery. It was Friday, January 7, 1898. Tributes poured in from all over the South and from the rank and file of the Presbyterian Church.

His widow had this monument erected with two inscriptions:

ROBERT LEWIS DABNEY, M.A., D.D., LL.D.

Born March 5, 1820.
Died January 3, 1898.

Minister of the Gospel, Professor of Theology in Union Seminary, and of Philosophy in the University of Texas, Major in the Confederate Army, and Chief of Staff to Stonewall Jackson.

DABNEY

In unshaken loyalty of devotion to his friends, his country, and his religion, firm in misfortune, ever active in earnest endeavor, he labored all his life for what he loved with a faith in good cause, that was ever one with his faith in God.

VI

MOSES DRURY HOGE

Many people have been tracing their roots. The oldest reference to the name Hoge goes back to 1425. It is thought that the family came to England from Normandy.[1]

About the close of the seventeenth century, William Hoge came to the colonies. He apparently was a man of means. He crossed the Atlantic to escape the religious persecutions of the Stuarts. William traveled from Perth-Amboy to Delaware, and then to the Cumberland Valley in Pennsylvania. Here his eldest son John founded the village of Hogestown.[2]

William moved further south to Frederick County, Virginia. He gave land for the old Opequon Church "the first place of worship in the Valley of Virginia."[3] William lived to be ninety years of age, and watched his children and grandchildren grow to be prominent persons.

A younger Moses Hoge founded the Presbyterian Church in Shepherdstown, and spent twenty years there. Then he moved to Hampden-Sydney and gave another thirteen years of his life to the training of theological students. Dr. John Rice is usually considered to be the founder of the school which has since moved to Richmond and is known as Union Theological Seminary,[4] but Hoge deserves a large share of honor too.

"Before the days of the railroads, Hampden-Sydney was on the great highway from Washington to the South. . . . Prince Edward Court House was just a mile away."[5] Patrick Henry and John Randolph were often seen there. In fact, Dr. Hoge often gave the students a holiday on court day, feeling they could learn so much from John Randolph.

Samuel Davis Hoge, a son of Dr. Moses Hoge, wooed and won Elizabeth Rice Lacy. They were married in February of 1817. At the time, he was pastor of Bethesda Church at Culpeper Court House. Part time was also given to a congregation at Madison Court House, and at Germanna. Funds were slack, so he came to Hampden-Sydney as a professor, and for a time as vice-president of the college.

The marriage is full of genealogical interest. Elizabeth was the daughter of Drury Lacy and Anne Smith. They had three sons. William and Drury became ministers, and Horace a physician. Judith married a minister, and Elizabeth entered the Hoge family.[6]

William Lacy was the father of Dr. Beverly Tucker Lacy whom we shall meet later as Jackson's unofficial chaplain, and of Major J. Horace Lacy, the owner of Chatham and Ellwood, and J. P. Smith's father-in-law.

Samuel and Elizabeth lived just west of the college building in a residence known as Steward's Hall. According to family tradition, a son was born there on the night of September 17, 1818. He was named after his two grandfathers, Moses Drury. Both of them were outstanding preachers, and young Moses was to be like them.

When Moses was just a toddler, his father resigned his teaching in Virginia, and the family moved to Ohio. Samuel Hoge served a church and taught at the University of Athens for several years. This seems to have been a Presbyterian center. The family of J. P. Smith was there later. Samuel died in 1826. This threw the family into dire financial straits. Mrs. Hoge took in boarders, washed, ironed, and did other chores in an effort to make enough money to keep the family together.

As the years passed, Moses grew tall and thin. He was to be that way all his life. At the tender age of sixteen, he rode horseback alone to North Carolina to live with an uncle. He survived the trip. There he prepared himself for college, and taught children who were almost as old as he was. Sessions were held in a one-room log building.

The year 1840 brought graduation from the campus of Hampden-Sydney where he had been born. R. L. Dabney had become one of his best friends. Their friendship was to continue throughout life. Hoge was a lot like Jackson. He led a Spartan type existence. He was thoroughly self-disciplined, and although good-natured, did not have time for horseplay. He also had self-confidence, and like Jackson, believed he could do anything he set out to do. He was an early riser. Most mornings found him up at 5:00 a.m. He lighted his candle and his fire, studied until breakfast, went to class until 2:00 p.m. and then cut wood for his fire. This regime led him to graduate with honors.

Three or four miles from Hampden-Sydney was Popular Hill, the home of James D. Wood. Hoge was a frequent visitor to Popular Hill. Moses became very interested in Susan Wood. They passed love notes by hiding them in a crack in the wall. One day while riding over the estate, Moses asked for Susan's hand in marriage. On March 20, 1844, they were married. Other than a long twenty-minute sermon by the clergyman, it was a joyous ceremony.[7]

"No man was happier in his married life than Dr. Hoge." Susan complemented him in every way. He was an excellent helpmate. Their life was full of sorrow though. His health was not good, and in the twenty-four years of their married life, Susan Hoge lost her parents, brother, five grown sisters, and four children in death. Many times she had to run the house alone. Moses in Europe or off on a speaking engagement.

In the spring of 1868 she was stricken with a fatal disease. Death came on February 23, 1869.[8]

With a father, two grandfathers, and four uncles already in the Christian ministry, it did not take Moses long to consider his next vocational step. He entered Union Theological Seminary, located at the time on the Hampden-Sydney Campus.

As he completed his seminary training, Moses considered several calls. One was from Alabama. But the one that seemed most challenging and exciting was a call from Richmond. Dr. William Swan Plumer was planning a mission church in Richmond. So Moses went to Richmond as

Dr. Plumer's assistant at First Presbyterian Church in the autumn of 1843. He was now twenty-five years of age.

He was a man full of energy, and soon a mission church was going quite well on Fifth Street. Sixty-three names were on the first church roll, and even though it was at the western edge of the city of Richmond, the congregation grew rapidly. They were held spellbound by the boy preacher. A larger church was built, but a depression came, and Hoge donated his salary to keep things going. He supported himself by operating a school for girls.

Then the clouds lifted. A great spiritual revival blessed the church, and Hoge along with the congregation was going full speed ahead once again.

Speaking of sailing, Hoge loved to travel. He preached to large congregations on the East Coast. And in 1854 crossed the Atlantic. He made fifteen additional trips during his life, traveling on several occasions with his friend, Dr. Hunter McGuire.

When the Civil War broke out, Moses had a lot of soul searching to do. During the Mexican War he applied for a chaplaincy post, but was not assigned. At that time he carefully wrote out the reasons he should go and minister to the soldiers.

However, that had been thirteen years ago. Things were different now. He was a little older. He had a large church in the main city of the Confederacy, and his wife was not in good health. Soldiers and politicians were flocking to the city. He had a ministry right in Richmond.

One of the sad things about the "tragic era" is the large amount of boys and young men entering the service. Hoge's initial encounter with this situation was with a company of students from Hampden-Sydney. They were led by Dr. J. M. P. Atkinson, president of the college and now a company commander. Hoge had Atkinson preach at Second Church. Thirty of the company took Holy Communion. Moses preached at the camps, several times on Sunday, and often during the week.

Soon he became friends with President Jefferson Davis,

Joseph E. Johnston, Robert E. Lee, many cabinet and government officials and soldiers in the ranks.

Vice-President Stephens asked Hoge to become chaplain of the Confederate Congress. Thus every day at noon, he went to the Capitol to pray for the governing body.

Hoge's exposure to combat came when he made a trip on horseback to visit the battlefield of Seven Pines. He saw the horror and heroism of battle. He saw dead lying by the roadside and heard the groaning of the wounded and dying. He tried to comfort the wounded and prayed with many.

Jackson arrived in the Richmond area on June 25, and took part in the battles which drove McClellan from the gates of the city.

After the campaign, Jackson and his men rested for a while near Westover, and then moved closer to Richmond on the Mechanicsville Road. On Sunday, July 13, Jackson rode into Richmond. He had a busy day, visiting the mother of a fallen member of his command, and a strategy conference with Lee and President Davis. However, on this his first visit to Richmond since gaining fame in the Shenandoah Valley he went to hear Dr. Hoge preach at the Second Presbyterian Church. If Hunter McGuire is right, he fell asleep. This was amazing, because "no one slept on Hoge."

When the service was over, Jackson slipped quietly out of the church. Today a marker placed by the United Daughters of the Confederacy is on the end of the pew. Jackson wrote, "I heard Rev. Dr. M. D. Hoge preach in his church, and also in the camp of the Stonewall Brigade. It is a great comfort to have the privilege of spending a quiet Sabbath within the walls of a house dedicated to the service of God."[9]

Jackson also gave Hoge a pass which read "Permit the bearer, the Rev. Moses D. Hoge, D.D., to pass at pleasure from Richmond to any part of my command and return to the city."

Hoge used the pass in the afternoon. James P. Smith tells us, "Dr. Hoge drove out to preach in the camp of the Stonewall Brigade. How well I remember the great assembly of young soldiers, seated on the ground like the five thousand at Bethsaida in companies,. . . ."[10]

Dr. White says, "He knew well how to present the solemn appeal, urging the soldiers as they entered the field of battle to put their trust in the God of their fathers. . . . Many were persuaded by his preaching to accept the Christian faith; many . . . were strengthened by his exhortation to stand like men in the hour of danger."

During the Civil War, Bibles were very scarce in the South. The publishing houses printing Bibles were located in the North. Jackson and Dr. Hoge discussed this painful lack. The Virginia Bible Society had distributed all it had in stock. The folks in Richmond, Nashville, and Charleston responded to Dr. Hoge's appeal, and sent Bibles for the soldiers. However, there was still a great need.

Hoge, his brother William, and R. L. Dabney talked and prayed about the situation. Southern ports were blockaded by Union vessels. Trusting in the Lord, though, Dr. Hoge decided to run the blockade, seeking to reach England and obtain Bibles there. It was a dangerous undertaking, but the preachers felt it had to be done. The need was great, they were risking their lives, he could not do less.

In absolute secrecy, Dr. Hoge sailed from Charleston, South Carolina. In fact, it was a thrilling adventure. Moses wrote:

> Our run through the blocking squadron was glorious. I was in the severest and bloodiest battles fought around Richmond; but it was not more exciting than that midnight adventure, when amid lowering clouds and dashes of rain, and just enough wind to get up commotion in the sea to drown out the noise of our paddle wheels we darted along, with all lights extinguished, and not even a cigar burning on deck, until we were safely out, and free from the Federal fleet.

Reaching London, Hoge went to see Lord Shaftesbury, the president of the British and Foreign Bible Society. Shaftesbury responded with 10,000 Bibles, 50,000 Testaments, and 250,000 Scriptural booklets of the Psalms and Gospels. These were placed on several ships, so that if one was sunk or captured, the others might get through. Most of the Bibles reached Confederate lines.

Moses had a narrow escape coming home. Near Wil-

Second Presbyterian Church, Richmond.

mington, North Carolina, his ship was spotted by Union vessels. They gave chase, firing as they sped near. The Confederate blockade runner barely managed to reach the protecting guns of Fort Fisher. Then she became stuck on a sandbar.

When Hoge left for England, he carried a letter of recommendation from none other than Judah P. Benjamin, the Confederate secretary of state. It read:

> Mr. Hoge, who is one of our most eloquent and accomplished divines, devotes himself to the effort to supply our Sunday Schools and camps books of religious instruction, which our own press is now unable to furnish in consequence of the vast diversion of peaceful labor from its ordinary pursuits.

After he returned, Hoge was most gratified with the response to his efforts. They came from the private soldiers who were grateful for the Bibles, and from generals and other leaders. The officers apparently had been presented with Bibles.

> I . . . pray that I may be able to practice its holy teachings. The success which attended your expedition and the number of books of Scripture you procured is subject of devout thanksgiving to God, and hearty congratulation to yourself.
>
> R. E. Lee

R. S. Ewell conveyed his thanks along with the hope, a request to Hoge to join him in prayer "that I may be assisted in following the precepts of the Divine Word, and that I may be guided by its wisdom."

James P. Smith delivered a Bible to Robert E. Rodes. The Bible gave him great pleasure. Rodes said, "I will prize it highly, and read it, I hope, with profit to my soul."

Sandie Pendleton gave a Bible to Jeb Stuart, the cavalry officer. Jeb sent thirty-six dollars for testaments and tracts to be given to his friends. Joseph E. Johnston, a close friend of Hoge's, states, "I assure you that no gift has ever afforded me so much gratification."

Moses Drury Hoge had done well. He had a lot to think about. Queen Victoria had commanded him to preach in her presence. She was so grateful she offered him a present. He refused, but asked if he could have some sprigs of ivy from Westminster Abbey. These were given, brought across the Atlantic, and planted in the courtyard of Second Presbyterian Church.

After Mary Anna Jackson left Yerby's to return home, she stopped at the Richmond home of Dr. and Mrs. Drury. In the midst of morning devotions on May 3, she received the news from her brother that Tom had fallen at Chancellorsville. She waited anxiously at the Hoge's until it was safe to head for Guiney Station. When she went, Mrs. Hoge went with her. The preacher's wife was with her the day Thomas Jonathan Jackson "crossed over the river." And Anna tells the vivid story of how she awakened in her grief on May 10, the room filled with moonlight, alone in her sorrow with the exception of Little Julia and Mrs. Hoge sleeping in the room with her.

Brother William wrote to Moses about the Jackson funeral train. He apparently was in Gordonsville.

> About ten minutes after our train arrived, the special train came slowly around the curve, bearing its sad, precious burden, the dead body of our beloved glorious Jackson. As it drew near, the minute guns, the soldier's funeral bell, sounded heavily. . . . As the train stopped, I caught sight of the coffin, wrapped in the flag he had borne so so high. . . . Many wreaths of exquisite flowers, too, covered it from head to foot. Sitting near the body were young Morrison, our dear friend Jimmy Smith, and Major Pendleton.[11]

Smith asked Hoge to get in and ride with them to Charlottesville. Hoge asked if it might be possible to see Mrs. Jackson. Smith assured him that it would be alright. Hoge was impressed with her bearing, and how she was holding up. William stooped over and kissed little Julia. He writes: "She was . . . evidently bearing all and doing all as she felt that her husband could have wished her to do, that she seemed to me just what he would have been in her place – the tender, helpless, stricken, brave little wife of such a saint, such a hero. She spoke of the pleasure he had had in my visit to camp." (This was at Moss Neck earlier in the year.)

William told his brother that Mrs. Jackson had gone to

Governor Letcher's in late April and then to Susan's (Dr. Hoge's home) to be more quiet. She learned of Tom's wound on Monday, but could not get to him until Thursday.

In the midst of all of this, Moses received more sad news. His son Lacy, his pride and joy, had died. The two had been extremely close. This was a crushing blow.

During the war, most of the Confederate leaders worshipped at one time or another at Second Church. Dr. Hoge spent much time ministering to the wounded in the military hospitals. And the congregation tried to give aid to those who were discharged and unable to resume military duty. At times, the Lecture Hall of the church was filled with wounded. On one occasion, there were thirty-five men in the room awaiting transfer to another facility.

During the evacuation of Richmond, the manse and part of the church caught fire, but were saved. When the magazine blew up, the buildings rocked, and the church windows blown out.

Poor Mrs. Hoge faced this alone, and conveyed the news to her husband via letter. He had accompanied President Davis and the cabinet when they left Richmond. He had been a spokesman for the Confederacy, and took the final defeat very hard. When he returned to the city a month later, he said, "Our overthrow is the worst thing that could have happened for the South."

But like all good men, he got over his depression, and went about the task of putting things together again. He corresponded with General Lee in Lexington about education, and was soon editing several literary and educational papers.

Calls came from Saint Louis, Baltimore, Nashville, and other large cities. Many churches wanted him for their pastor. However, his allegiance was to Richmond, and Virginia.

In 1873 he delivered an oration at the unveiling of the Jackson Statue in Richmond. Many feel this was his greatest speech, although he was in great demand, and gave many talks.

129

Mrs. Jackson was greatly pleased at Hoge's oration. Writing to the preacher she said, "I have read it carefully twice, and with new pleasure each time. . . . I wish you could know how much I value your true appreciation of the exalted character of my sainted husband."

Wishing you and yours every blessing, I am,
Most truly your friend,
M. A. Jackson

D. H. Hill summarized the address:

> Dr. Hoge made the mighty effort of his life. He was inspired by the grandeur of the occasion, by the vastness of the audience, and above all by the greatness of the subject of his eulogy. He impressed all who heard him that he is the most eloquent orator on this continent. . . .
>
> Dr. Hoge, in closing his address, alluded to the prophecy of Jackson, that the time would come when his men would be proud that they belonged to the Stonewall Brigade. Rising to his full height, the orator exclaimed in his clear, ringing tones, "Men of the Stonewall Brigade, that time has come. Behold the image of your illustrious commander!" The veil was raised, the life-like statue stood revealed, recalling so vividly the loved form of the illustrious soldier that tears rained down ten thousand faces. Men of sternest natures, cast iron men, were weeping like children.[12]

This was the second big event of the year for Hoge. Earlier he had been sent to the General Assembly of the Presbyterian Church. The delegates chose him as moderator.

It would be impossible to list the Confederate memorial addresses, the funerals for old soldiers, and leading statesmen, and the prayers he gave on public occasions. He was called across the nation to give the sermon at the dedication of new churches. Thus, he spoke in Atlanta, Saint Louis, Louisville, and many other places.[13]

Reading the sermons and prayers of Dr. Hoge, one can see that he had a way with words. This was very evident at a commencement at Hampden-Sydney after the war. R. L. Dabney spoke one day, and Hoge the next.

Mrs. Jackson and little Julia were in the audience. Dabney had spoken on "The New South." Hoge talked about the governor of Virginia lifting little Julia upon the platform, presenting her to the crowd while cheers rent the air. "Why?" said Hoge. "General Jackson is dead but his daughter still lives. The Old South is dead, but the New South is alive, maybe slender and frail like the little girl, but alive and well." Cheers filled the air. Hoge was hardly able to continue. He had made his point with a dramatic illustration.

A man does not occupy one pulpit for fifty-four years without having a lot of commitment. Hoge, like the other preachers close to Jackson, knew the Lord. He knew the lure and power of sin. But he knew the grace of the Lord Jesus. He knew the power of the Holy Spirit. And he preached the message, "Behold the Lamb of God that taketh away the sin of the world."

The lives of those connected with Jackson are closely intertwined. McGuire and Hotchkiss maintained their relationship after the war, while Hoge and McGuire traveled together, especially to Europe. He had an audience with the Crown Princess of Denmark, and was called to her office to talk with her about raising children according to the teaching of Scripture.

He and McGuire talked often. And on Sunday night, although he was an Episcopalian, Hunter McGuire drove Hoge to church. Washington and Lee awarded him an honorary degree, and he became a trustee of educational Hampden-Sydney College, and a director of many other charitable groups.

On February 26, 1895, he was honored in Richmond's Masonic Temple. It was one of the largest gatherings in the city's history. Thousands from all walks of life, and from many groups came to pay him homage. It was a great moment for Jackson's friend.

On November 4, 1898, Dr. Hoge went to see a bereaved family in the congregation. In the dusk, he pulled his buggy into the path of an oncoming streetcar and was badly injured. Complications set in, and death came two months later.

On the afternoon of January 5, Dr. Hoge was very restless. Towards evening he fell into deep sleep, but then

131

awakened. His daughter was by his side saying, "Jesus is with you." At times she repeated the words of the hymn, "I heard the voice of Jesus say," and the Twenty-third Psalm. About 10:00 p.m. he called her name and then spoke no more. He was gone.[14]

He had directed that his services be held with utmost simplicity. The casket was covered with plain black cloth. Dr. James P. Smith offered one of the prayers. The hymns, prayers, and Scriptures were full of inspiration and hope. Then sobbing broke out in the church. His body was carried from the church he had served for fifty-four years. Thousands lined the street outside.

Before dark, he was resting in Hollywood Cemetery. Hoge had conducted hundreds of services in the cemetery. Now the words were being said for him. He was buried among "the great and heroic dead of the Confederacy; . . . in the soil of that Virginia he had so loyally served and so devotedly loved"; by the noble James River that sings the requiem of the dead.

Hoge had a policy of never dating a letter at the beginning of a new year without feeling some emotion. Maybe he realized that he would go home at the beginning of a year and experience a life without end in the presence of his Lord.[15] For many years, Moses Drury Hoge "was an institution and Richmond would not be the same without him."

VII

ABNER HOPKINS
CHAPLAIN OF THE STONEWALL BRIGADE

Abner C. Hopkins was born in Powhatan County, Virginia, on October 24, 1835. He attended Hampden-Sydney College, graduating in 1855. Needing money, he taught school for two years, and then entered the Presbyterian Seminary, located on the campus of his alma mater. One of the members of the faculty was R. L. Dabney, who like Hopkins, was soon to be associated with Thomas Jonathan Jackson.

Following graduation, Hopkins was called to a Presbyterian Church in Martinsburg, at the northern end of the Shenandoah Valley. He was installed on December 6, 1861.[1] The following May, he married Anne P. Atkinson, daughter of another Presbyterian minister, then serving in Winchester.

Hopkins did not enter the war until late spring of that year. He may have postponed entry due to his marriage. On the other hand, Abner states that he waited because chaplains were held in low esteem and respect.

Jackson was already heavily engaged in the Valley campaign. Hopkins was commissioned in the Second Virginia Infantry and overtook the unit between Franklin and McDowell.

"The Rapidity and fighting of the Valley campaign caused most of the Chaplain's work to be done with the wounded."[2] At the invitation of the regimental commander, Hopkins held nightly prayer meetings, and preached several times on Sunday.

At the time, there was little organization or cooperation among the chaplains. In fact, Hopkins says that he served three months with the Stonewall brigade before he ever met a fellow minister. Until Second Manassas, there seems to have been little religious interest in the Stonewall brigade.

On August 28 during the initial fighting at Second Manassas, Colonel Botts of the Second Virginia fell. The next evening at the close of the action, Hopkins fell asleep under a tree. He was awakened by Colonel W. H. Baylor, the current commander of the brigade. "Chaplain," the officer asked, "Do you feel too tired to conduct a prayer meeting. I feel grateful to God for sparing my life today, and would like the brigade to gather for prayer."

No chaplain declines such a request. Hopkins was up in a moment. From the bivouac area of the Second Virginia, and the other regiments of the Stonewall brigade, came the tired officers and men to pray. Among them was Captain Hugh White, the son of Jackson's pastor. "White and others led in prayer. A solemn meeting was enjoyed by all." Sadly, it was the last prayer meeting for many of those present.

The next day, both Baylor and White fell upon the field of conflict. "The evening's sun set upon the corpses of two noble and generous men, Baylor and White. . . . I would express my hope that their mingled service is continued in heaven."[3]

Then it was northward to Maryland. After camping near Frederick, Maryland, Robert E. Lee and the Army of Northern Virginia moved westward on September 10. Jackson and Hopkins rode together on the National Pike, crossing Catoctin Mountain heading for Middletown. Stonewall expressed his hope that the men were prepared at all times to meet their maker. He also stated that he hoped Colonel Baylor was prepared to meet God.

Late in November, Franklin Paxton, a resident of Lexington, and a member of Jackson's church, took command of the Stonewall brigade. Paxton said that "from now on, there will be no furloughs for the chaplains." They were too badly needed.

134

When the Stonewall brigade went into winter camp at Moss Neck, near Fredericksburg, Paxton urged Hopkins to complete a chapel for the Stonewall brigade. He even sent volunteers to aid the work. The chapel was finished early in January. For several months, this would be Hopkins's home pulpit. Jackson was often present at the services.[4]

In the city of Fredericksburg, the great revival was under way. It had started in the camp at Bunker Hill. And it continued under the preaching of Beverly Lacy and others. Hopkins normally had a full church himself.

With all the religious interest, it was necessary for the chaplains to organize and plan some unified work. Lacy was selected to lead the group of chaplains from the Second Corps. And Abner Hopkins, chaplain of the Stonewall brigade, sent out the note requesting all the chaplains to meet at Round Oak Baptist Church on March 16, 1863.

During the winter, Hopkins and Paxton became very close friends. The brigade commander made a profession of faith, and just prior to the battle of Chancellorsville, he rode to talk with Hopkins. He told the minister that he did not believe he would survive the next battle. He did not want to go unprepared. The two men prayed, and Paxton's premonition was indeed correct.

In January, Hopkins organized a Bible study group in the Second Virginia. Soon he had thirty men. "By the latter part of February a very general interest in religion was spread throughout the brigade. Chaplains were more devoted; congregations larger, . . . chaplains of the brigade and division began to grow acquainted, interested in each other and cooperative." Some of the chaplains went to see Jackson about prayer meetings and conferences. He was encouraging.[5]

Sunday, February 29, 1863, Hopkins was all set to preach from Revelation 3:2. After the service had begun, Brother Walton introduced Jones to Hopkins. With some reluctance, Abner invited John to bring the message. J. William brought just about the same message Hopkins had prepared although from another text. This made Abner feel the meeting and the sermons were providential. These two

135

messages, one by Jones in the morning, and the other by Hopkins in the afternoon, seem to mark a turning point in religious life at Moss Neck. Christians began praying and things began to happen.

During the week, B. T. Lacy arrived on the scene. He preached with fine results. And the request of Hopkins and the other chaplains about an organization was presented to Lacy and then confirmed by Jackson. "Rev. William J. Hoge was also sent by the good Lord; he preached; and the wave of interest rolled on."[6]

Hopkins continues by saying:

> Soon sinners began to inquire the way to God; Christians began to make unusual efforts in winning souls; solemnity characterized the command, and congregations began to exceed the capacity of our primitive house of worship. . . . Cold professors were revived; and sinners were converted; yet the work was silent, quiet and deep.[7]

The greatest work seems to have been in the Fourth Virginia. Hopkins's unit gave $140.00 for religious reading material. The Second also gave $505.25 for the relief of the suffering citizens of Fredericksburg. The men of Fourth contributed $349.75.

R. L. Dabney was asked to write two tracts, "Profane Swearing," and "Christ Our Substitute." These were published and distributed among the troops.

Beverly Lacy was able to work out the details for a meeting of the chaplains. (More about that in the chapter about him.) Hopkins wrote the notice that was sent to all chaplains, calling a meeting on March 16 at Round Oak Baptist Church. The Reverend Mr. Vass and Hopkins took it to Jackson's headquarters. It was approved, and the meeting occurred.

Hopkins, like all the chaplains, had a lot of sad tasks during the war. Many of them were involved in ministering to the dying, and to the relatives of the soldiers.

Abner was ill with typhoid fever during the fighting at Chancellorsville. He was being treated in a home, and then hurried away to another place of safety to avoid capture by the Yankees. This happened on the day before Jackson

136

died. In writing to the wife of General Paxton, Hopkins states that due to illness:

> I could not be with him on that ill fated day, and have nothing of his last words to send you for comfort. I know, however, that he died as a brave, patriotic soldier, whose home and family are invaded and humiliated by an enemy, would prefer to die, doing his duty for their defence. . . .
>
> I can boast no claim to the special confidence of your husband. What I can tell you, you may have learned before from his own pen or tongue. But I am assured that you will be much comforted to learn that in every conversation with me for months past he has given evidence of very serious reflection on the subject of religion; and so great has been his zeal in encouraging chaplains in the religious instruction of his troops, that I am induced to hope that the blood of Christ has purchased his soul, and that he is among the rejoicing saints in the light.
>
> During my illness he kindly came to see me twice, the last time but a few days before the battle; and each time he introduced and continued to speak on religious matters. He always proved himself the chaplain's warm friend so long as he endeavored to promote the spiritual interest of his regiment and proved faithful to his ministerial office. . . .
>
> May the great Comforter administer to you all the consolation which Heaven bestows on earth, and be so good a Guide and Light to your fatherless children as to compensate for their great bereavement.[8]

This letter from Chaplain Hopkins was written on May 12.

Hopkins missed Gettysburg due to illness. Then in the summer of 1863, Hopkins preached many times in the camps near Madison and Orange Court Houses. The main camp during the winter was at Mount Pisgah Church near Raccoon Ford, five miles northeast of Orange Court House. In this camp, Hopkins went to his commander and obtained his efforts in checking the sale of liquor by the sutler.

During the Wilderness action, Hopkins was ordered by Dr. McGuire to assist him in the care of the wounded. It was during this battle of course that the Stonewall brigade was just about wiped out, many of the men being captured and sent to Fort Delaware.

Later in 1864, Hopkins joined General Gordon at New

Market. Drunkenness and profanity were major problems. Late in the fall, Gordon was ordered to Petersburg, and Hopkins went with him. The two became good friends.

March 9 was set as a National Fast Day in the Confederacy. The night before, Hopkins announced that he was going to have a special service for those using profanity. One bright young man told the chaplain he should have a full house. He did. Some stood outside in the rain. "Family worship" was held at Gordon's headquarters much like at Jackson's. Hopkins was with the army until the very end at Appomattox, and on the day of surrender talked with two chaplains from the Union army. They were amazed how little Hopkins had made. They had been paid $130 and two horses.

The words of J. William Jones describe what Hopkins experienced so often in the war.

> No church bell summons, to gorgeous houses of worship, elegant ladies or fashionably attired men. But a few taps of the drum, a few strains of the bugle, or better still, the singing of some familiar hymn, serves as a "church-call" well understood, and from every part of the camp weather-beaten soldiers, in faded and tattered uniforms, hasten to the selected spot and gather close around the preacher, who, with "Nature's great temple" for his church, and the blue canopy of heaven for his "soundingboard," is fortunate if he so much has a barrel or well rounded stump for a pulpit.[9]

On the other hand there were the brigade chapels. And in Fredericksburg, troops broke ranks to run to the Episcopal and Presbyterian churches, knowing that the first to arrive would get the seats. As we shall see in the chapter on Lacy, the churches were packed. The men were stirred "with a desire to hear the Gospel."

The clear voice of the singer reminds the men of home and loved ones. The chaplain does not tell the Lord the news of the day. He does not dwell on the cause of the South. But he talks about spiritual needs, and what the Lord can do. He begs for the Holy Spirit to move with convicting and converting power. Soon tears can be seen in the eyes of the men. And when the invitation to accept Christ is given, twenty and sometimes two hundred move forward to experience the new birth.[10]

Hopkins was low-keyed, yet veterans of the Stonewall brigade remembered several vivid pictures of the chaplain. Once in the heat of action, he grabbed a musket and rushed to the front with the troops. On another occasion, he took off his cap and waved the men forward, acting as a cheerleader.

December 9, 1866, brought the beginning of a new relationship and experience for Hopkins. He was installed as pastor of the Charles Town Church. Thus he was going to the place where John Brown was tried, and the hometown of J. Welles Hawks, Jackson's commissary officer, and the home of George Baylor who was to write a noted Civil War book. This was also home for many men who had served in the Second Virginia Infantry, part of the First Virginia brigade, later known as the Stonewall brigade.

He soon became known and loved throughout the town and the countryside. As a hobby, he established a little woodworking shop, and was very good at making sleighs.

His family liked to tell stories of little embarrassing moments in his life. A gentleman in Charles Town asked Hopkins if he would conduct his funeral services when he died. To this Abner replied, "Why sure, I'd be delighted to do that." Later he realized what he had said and was sorry.[11]

Abner took the lead in getting a monument to the Confederate soldiers in the Charles Town Cemetery. And when he himself died, the entire town closed shops and businesses until after the funeral.

The church historian states:

> December 9, 1866, was a notable date for Charles Town, for on that day Dr. A. C. Hopkins, of revered memory entered upon the pastoral relation which he so beautifully sustained for nearly fifty years. In a recent Magazine I picked up the expression "Nothing is so difficult as the delineation of the soul of a people." Dr. Hopkins seemed as the soul not alone of the church, or of the town, but of the section to which he belonged. He was the soul of the South.[12]

July 21, 1891, marked the thirtieth anniversary of the First Battle of Manassas. Thousands gathered that day in Lexington. The occasion, the dedication of the Jackson monument in the cemetery where the general had been buried. The sculptor was Edward V. Valentine.

139

The Charles Town Presbyterian Church.

140

Abner C. Hopkins, chaplain of the Stonewall brigade.
Courtesy the Presbyterian Historical Foundation

It was a lovely summer day. The streets were filled with
old veterans and folks from across Virginia and the South.
The streets and buildings were decorated "in keeping with
Jackson's views—simple and plain, yet beautiful."

141

At the Virginia Military Institute, bunting and flags "of all descriptions floated from every conspicuous place." The general's former classroom was banked with flowers. His old chair and table were there. A blackboard bore the inscription, "He fought a good fight." Another panel stated, "Lieutenant General Jackson's body lay in state in this tower, May 14, 1863."

To accommodate the crowds, the exercises were held on the campus of Washington and Lee University. The Old Rockbridge Artillery Band opened the proceedings with music. Then Dr. A. C. Hopkins, known as "the Fighting Chaplain" of the Stonewall brigade, offered an "eloquent prayer."

Following the prayer General Wade Hampton introduced one of Jackson's lieutenants, Jubal A. Early. "Old Jube" delivered a very moving address. After which, the crowd moved to the cemetery. The military procession formed in an adjoining field. They formed a phalanx of veterans.

A little platform was beside the statue. Mrs. Jackson and her two small grandchildren were on the platform. When the signal gun sounded, the two little children pulled the cord, and the veil fell. "The statue of the great Jackson stood revealed to the admiring gaze of the thousands around it." Gunners from the Rockbridge Artillery fired fifteen rounds. The shots came from a cannon used at First Manassas. The air was rent once again with the famous "Rebel Yell." The sounds echoed from the hills of Lexington. It was a great day in Lexington, and Abner Hopkins, the former chaplain of the Stonewall brigade, was a part of it.

The Winchester Presbytery paid tribute to Hopkins by saying:

> It was as Chaplain that some of his most effective work was done. His cool bravery in time of battle, his signal indifference to danger, his unremitting attention to both the temporal and spiritual wants of the soldiers, the cheerfulness with which he shared in all their hardships, privations and peril, endeared him to them as an ideal friend, and won for him their profound and lasting admiration and love.

That devotion did not end with the war. During the remaining years of his life, soldiers from the Stonewall brigade and from the Army of Northern Virginia frequently came to Dr. Hopkins for help. He never turned anyone away. Often he gave them money from his own pocket.

In Charles Town, his "ministry was distinguished as few others have been, by an untiring devotion on his part to the spiritual welfare of his people." His efforts were awarded by their loyalty "that grew in intensity to the last. . . . He was a model of Christian manhood. . . . He was a humble child of God." And he was a friend of Thomas J. Jackson.

Death came to Abner C. Hopkins on December 4, 1911, "on the 50th anniversary of the organization of the Southern Presbyterian Church, and was buried December 6, the 51st anniversary of his ordination to the ministry."

"The memory of his noble life will remain fresh and green in the hearts of the people whom, with intense devotion, he served so long; and in the hearts of his brethren whom he served so well."[13]

VIII

BEVERLY TUCKER LACY

Lacy was one of the best known chaplains in the Army of Northern Virginia. He served as the unofficial chaplain of the Second Corps, and was very close to Jackson, often sharing his quarters. After Jackson's death, Lacy continued in this capacity with R. S. Ewell, and Jubal Early.

Tucker, as he was generally known, was a "pk" or preacher's kid, the son of Rev. William S. Lacy and Sallie Graham Lacy. He was born in Prince Edward County, Virginia, on February 19, 1819.[1] "His mother was the daughter of Edward Graham of Lexington, . . . and niece of William Graham, principal and founder of Liberty Hall Academy," the school which later became Washington College. In 1821, the Lacys moved to Saint Louis. However, their stay was brief. They moved again to Somerville, Tennessee. Here Tucker grew up, and left for Lexington to attend Washington College. He and his brother graduated in 1843.[2]

From Lexington, Tucker traveled to Princeton and Theological Seminary. Upon completion of his studies he returned to the Shenandoah Valley, and served in Winchester at the Old School Church, from 1847 to 1851. The ten years prior to the war found him in Salem, Virginia, and Frankfort, Kentucky.

While in Winchester, Lacy married Agnes Reid Alexander of Lexington. To this union a son, John Alexander Lacy, was born. Sadly, Mrs. Lacy only lived four years after her marriage to the young theologian. The little son was raised by her parents in Lexington.

144

Although he admired pretty women, and apparently fell deeply in love with young Georgia Bryan, Tucker never remarried.

His brother Horace prospered and bought the lovely Chatham estate on the banks of the Rappahannock near Fredericksburg. Tucker met Miss Bryan on a visit to Chatham. Horace wrote to Aunt Lizzie Graham about the episode:

> Tucker spent Tuesday with me and preached at night. No man for years has produced a greater sensation in the community than Tucker on his visit here. He is a noble preacher. I feel sorry for him and almost regret he met Georgia Bryan. I do not think she will marry him.[3]

Horace had good reasons to feel this way. Georgia was young and lovely, with many suitors. Tucker was old enough to be her father, and had nothing to offer on the salary of a preacher.

Tucker was known, loved, and respected in the churches and communities where he served. However, like Jackson, it took the Civil War to bring him to prominence.

After First Manassas, the South thought victory was sure. They were elated, thinking one victory had won the war. England and France would come to their aid, and then independence. However, this did not happen. Despair set in, and along with it, the common vices of wartime: drunkenness, gambling, profanity, and the like.[4]

Reverses in the spring of 1862 at Roanoke Island and at Shiloh started a movement toward God, and by the fall of 1862, many revivals were occurring in the camps. Soldiers had seen loved ones fall. They knew they might be next. They wanted to prepare their soul and get right with God. A man who helped them to do this was Tucker Lacy.

By late December 1862 Jackson was at Moss Neck, and the Second Corps encamped on a line southeast of Fredericksburg. Many of the regiments in his command were without chaplains. Jackson was deeply concerned about this as he felt responsible for their spiritual welfare. In fact, fourteen North Carolina regiments in the Second Corps were without chaplains.

For a time, Jackson thought of inviting Dr. Benjamin M. Palmer of New Orleans to come and be a missionary chaplain to the Second Corps. Meanwhile, Beverly T. Lacy had come to Fredericksburg.

According to Marsena Patrick, Union forces were in possession of the town by May 12. Patrick became very angry over the Union soldiers entering and stealing from private homes. He took stern measures to protect against this. And he writes, "Officers became very devotional all of a sudden and swarmed over here for Church—I had intended to go to Mr. Lacy's Church (the Presbyterian) myself." McDowell and his staff came as a group to the service. "We wonder what Lacy preached about."[5]

Patrick's headquarters were in the building, now occupied by a bank just across from the church. It was called the "Herndon House," taking its name from the first cashier of the bank who lived in the house.

The church itself is quite historic. And in 1862 the president of the United States had stood on the steps of the bank and addressed the troops and the local residents during his visit to the area.

Both Winchester and Fredericksburg suffered a lot during the war. Jane Howison Beale has left an unpublished diary describing the horrors of 1862 and in her beloved city. The folks needed to hear Lacy's sermon on May 4, 1862. His text was, "Lo, I am with you always." The people needed to be reassured that God had not forsaken them during their suffering.[6]

On June 29 it was raining, and there was a Union service with the Methodists and Presbyterians. Federal soldiers attended and listened with much interest. Mrs. Beale hoped that the message might lead them to treat the people in a kindlier manner.

All through the summer the Federal soldiers came in large numbers to hear the Reverend Mr. Rogers, the Methodist minister, and also the Reverend Mr. Lacy. The latter's sermons "were popular both with members of the occupying forces and with the townspeople who still remained."[7]

September 18, the day after the Battle of Sharpsburg, had

146

been proclaimed as a "Day of Thanksgiving" by Jefferson Davis. This was in gratitude for the victories at Second Manassas. Mr. Lacy preached from the text, "The Lord has done great things for us, whereof we are glad."[8]

After Antietam, George McClellan was relieved of command, and Ambrose Burnside was placed in charge of the Union Army of the Potomac. It was time for another advance on Richmond. And Fredericksburg stood in the way. By late November, the banks of the Rappahannock were filled with men in blue. Chatham, the Lacy home, was occupied by Union generals.

On November 21, Burnside demanded the surrender of Fredericksburg. Lee said, "No." Burnside then prepared to shell the city.

General Lee advised the poor civilians to leave. He even sent some wagons and ambulances to transport the women and the children. It may have been during this period that James P. Smith's future wife left the area. The stream of refugees which Jackson saw when he arrived near Fredericksburg filled him with great sadness. Salem Church was filled with the poor unfortunate victims. We have seen pictures from Vietnam, but in November and December of 1862, the same thing occurred at Fredericksburg.

The situation calmed and people thought that they might escape without a battle or destruction. However, on December 11, Burnside commenced firing at daylight with 176 cannon placed on Stafford Heights. Throughout the day, the cannon belched forth fire and smoke. Forty homes in Fredericksburg were destroyed. Shells can still be seen imbedded in many structures including the Presbyterian Church where Lacy and Smith preached.

The Reverend Mr. Lacy sought refuge in the basement of a house with many others. There on his knees he prayed for God's protection and led the folks in repeating Psalm 27, "Though a host should encamp against me, my heart shall not fear." Then there was the sound of the shattering of glass, and the splintering of wood. A shell had hit Mrs. Beale's home. Her youngest son was stunned, but not seriously injured.[9]

147

Clara Barton stayed at the Lacy home at Chatham, and later crossed on a pontoon to minister to the Union wounded. She was appalled at "the city of death, its roofs riddled by shell, its very church a crowded hospital, every street a battle line."

This, of course, was December 13, during the heat of the action. She apparently ministered to the wounded at both the Episcopal and Presbyterian churches. "The memories of Fredericksburg remained with her distinct and terrible to the day of her death."

Perhaps no city suffered as much as Fredericksburg in December of 1862. Beverly Lacy was a part of that suffering, as was his congregation, and to a degree Jackson himself.[10]

A modern psychologist has written, "It's not what happens to you that's important, but how you handle the events that happen to you." We can break out in rebellion, or down in self-pity, or we can break through to God.

The suffering and disaster provided the background for a great spiritual awakening and revival on the banks of the Rappahannock, and instrumental in the revival were Lacy and Jackson.

Jackson and Lacy had already met, the first occasion was in Lexington in 1851. Then Lacy visited Jackson at his headquarters in Winchester in 1862.[11] Now the general summoned the preacher to headquarters at Moss Neck. Jackson invited Lacy to organize and supervise the work of chaplains. Tom was very apprehensive over the sins of the army and the people. He felt the lack of morality and spiritual commitment were hindering both the nation and the army. If Jackson could command "A converted army" he would feel secure. Tom felt so strongly about this that he offered to personally give two hundred dollars toward Lacy's salary, and to see that another three hundred would be available to give religious tracts to the soldiers.[12]

Lacy spent the night with the general. Together they prayed, and when moring came, Lacy told Jackson that he would have to consult the Presbyterian congregation in Fredericksburg.

In March, Lacy came to Moss Neck. He was commissioned a chaplain without assignment to any regiment. Sandie Pendleton, Jackson's chief of staff, writes on March 10:

> We have Tucker Lacy here with us . . . as a staff chaplain or Religious Director. . . . He is, except for constant conversational speech-making, quite an agreeable companion. The General has given him his finest horse, a blooded mare lately presented to him and he shares the General's room. He can do an earnest amount of good, if he sets earnestly to work at it in the right way.[13]

By March 22, Lacy had started regular family prayers or devotions at headquarters before breakfast. Sandie told his mother, "This is really quite a change in our mode of living."

The correspondent of the *Richmond Enquirer* wrote, "In portions of Gen. Jackson's corps, a very promising interest (in religion) is observed and the hearts of our Christian soldiers are much encouraged." The writer went on to say that Lacy was to work in the various regiments, and search for committed chaplains. "It is a wide field of usefulness, and we hope from the efforts of Mr. Lacy much good fruits to the glory of God."[14]

Jackson's hopes for the army and for Lacy's ministry were summarized in a letter to his pastor, Dr. White, whom we have already met:

> Each denomination of the Christian Churches throughout the South should send into the army some of its most prominent ministers who are distinguished for their piety, talents, and zeal; and such ministers should labor to produce concert of action among the chaplains and Christians in the army. These ministers should give special attention to preaching to regiments which are without chaplains, to let the regiments name the denomination from which they desire chaplains selected, and then to see that suitable chaplains are secured. A bad selection may prove a curse instead of a blessing. If a few prominent ministers thus connected with each army would cordially cooperate, I believe that glorious fruits would be the result. . . . I do not think that a chaplain, who would preach denominational sermons, should be in the army. His congregation is his regiment, and that is composed of persons of various denominations. I would like to see no question asked in the army as to what denomination a chaplain belongs, but let the question be, "Does He preach the Gospel?"[15]

To that any religious leader would have to say "Amen." This letter shows profound insight, and gives us great respect for the character and religious leadership of Jackson.

By the winter of 1862 the Army of Northern Virginia was ready for revival. The Stonewall brigade had already lost a large percentage of the men who reported for duty at Harpers Ferry. The soldiers realized that they could be stricken down at any time by enemy fire or disease.

Many chaplains were already working closely together. Lacy and Dr. William Hoge found a revival taking place in the ranks of Barksdale's Mississippi troops. Rev. W. B. Owen was their chaplain. He was a Methodist. For a time he was ably assisted by Dr. J. L. Burrows of the Baptist church. And one night, Dr. Hoge, a Presbyterian, preached after he was introduced by a Baptist minister. A Methodist chaplain was in charge of the service, and the meeting was held in the Episcopal Church, the largest one in Fredericksburg. "Old Jack" would have loved this type of an approach.[16]

Lacy may have talked a lot, but he was a man of action. He wanted, as Jackson had stated in his letter to Dr. White, the chaplains to work together. Therefore, a memo went out from headquarters of the Second Corps for all chaplains to gather at Round Oak Baptist Church in Caroline County. The church was near Moss Neck. The date set for the meeting was March 16. The purpose for the meeting was to establish "a Chaplains' Association of Jackson's Second Corps." This was done, and for the next eight weeks, or until May 19, 1863, the chaplains came together weekly to pray, study the Word, share victories, and problems. At the end of each session, Lacy was expected to make a report to General Jackson. This in itself is amazing. There may have been other generals who did this, but certainly few of the stature of Jackson. In response to good and positive reports Jackson would say, "That's good: we ought to thank God." So this is another dimension of the life and leadership of Jackson at Moss Neck and Yerby's.[17]

The general felt the chaplains should stay in service. He did not favor temporary duty. In his eyes, a chaplain had

Beverly Tucker Lacy

not only the patriotic, but Christian obligation to stay in the service. Leaves should be granted to the men of the cloth only in emergency. They should live with the regiment to which they were assigned and share the life of the men.

Lacy spelled out the primary duties of the chaplain, they discussed relationships with officers and men, and also the types of messages most needed by men far from home, constantly exposed to danger and death, and tempted by many things of the world.

Tucker Lacy practiced what he preached. On Saturday morning, April 4, 1863, he visited the Field Hospital of the Second Corps, located near Guiney Station. He spent some time in each ward, reading from the Bible, giving a short message, and then praying with the men.

From the hospital he went to the camp of John B. Gordon and then Georgia brigade. A service was already in progress. Lacy was invited to preach. Gordon, most of his staff, and many private soldiers were in attendance.[18]

In late March, after spending three months at Moss Neck, Jackson moved his headquarters to the home of Thomas Yerby. This was nearer Hamilton's Crossing.

Near the general's headquarters, an outdoor chapel was prepared. There were "rude seats and a temporary pulpit." Services were held in the open air. Jackson's presence encouraged the men in the ranks to attend. The general often sat under a tree, his eyes filling with delight as the men came to worship.

On one side of the seats, a tent was erected for the ladies who came to the services. Here in April of 1863 the wives of officers, and a few private soldiers came to the meetings.

This was almost hollowed ground for the Army of Northern Virginia. Under the bright blue sky, with breezes from the woods, the rank and file came to worship. Robert E. Lee and many of his lieutenants came, and of course T. J. Jackson was there, usually amidst the private soldiers. He listened intently, glad for the spirit of truth, and for the evidence of God at work in the army. "Never since the days when Whitfield preached to the mingled crowds of peers

152

and beggars in Moorefield, has the sky looked down upon a more imposing worship."[19]

Normally, Tucker Lacy was the preacher of the morning. He also led the Sunday evening services, prayer meetings on Wednesday, and met with Jackson for daily devotions. Sunday afternoons, the men met for hymn sings. Perhaps you can visit the spot, and visualize Jackson and men of the Second Corps singing, praying, and listening to the preaching of Tucker Lacy on the hill near Hamilton's Crossing.

Lacy says that April 5 was a lovely day, one of "singular beauty, just one for preaching in the open air." One thousand were present for the service.

> In [my] varied ministry I have seldom addressed so interesting and imposing an audience, and never one more respectful, solemn and tender. It was a noble sight to see there those, who led our armies to victory, and upon whom the eyes of the nation were turned with admiration and gratitude, melted in tears at the story of the cross and the exhibition of the love of God to the repenting and return sinner. Lee and staff, Jackson and staff, and many brigade and regimental officers were present. Some ladies were present in large tent nearby, and their voices mingled sweetly in the songs of Zion, with the deeper tones of the multitude. . . .[20]

This was Sunday, April 5, 1863, near Yerby's.

In the afternoon, Lacy conducted services in the bivouac area of Trimble's brigade.

Jackson was filled with delight to see the progress of the chaplain's meeting. These brought him in closer contact with the chaplains. He encouraged them to come to his quarters. They came to look upon him not only as their commander but also as a fellow Christian. Jackson desired a converted army. His theme was, "Duty is ours; consequences are God's." He was happy to have a Christian daily newspaper in the ranks.

At the meeting on April 14, 1863, the topic of discussion was, "Has there been enough preaching during active campaigns?" J. William Jones, chaplain of the Thirteenth Virginia, and the author of *Christ in Camp*, a must for all interested in the subject, introduced the topic.

Jones said that after the fighting around Richmond in the

153

summer of 1862, he assembled his decimated regiment. "Every officer and man was present. This was right under the guns of the enemy. At Second Manassas a shell fell in the midst of a service he was leading. No one was injured. The men scattered but reassembled.

William Nelson Pendleton, another *preacher Jackson knew,* was present at the meeting. He shared with the others how he had found large crowds at services just prior to big battles. He told the men there was no limit to what they could achieve if they just dedicated themselves to the effort. The fighting parson said that in addition to his military duties with the artillery, he had preached at least once every Sunday during the war.

Tucker Lacy told the men I "find it possible to preach under all circumstances. . . . Brethren, we are appointed to carry the spiritual bread of life to the men. We draw from a never failing supply. There is always enough, thank God. If we have some difficulties in getting it to the men in need, let us strive to do so. Difficulties prove their necessities. In the fighting many of these men must fall. One sermon more, brethren, for the love of souls, for the glory of God. Let us devise means to get this bread to them."

Lacy then urged the chaplains to be an example to all. They should go to the trenches, to the places where the men were and meet their spiritual needs; say to them, "I know you are ready to die for your country, but are you ready to meet your God?"[21]

Lacy urged the chaplains to visit the campfire, make friends with the men, let them know who they were. He said, "Earnest prayer by the campfire makes men rest better, and march better."

Tucker had some practical words of advice. He applied the Bible injunction, "They shall not be heard for their much speaking." He told the preachers, "Let brevity mark your sermons. Let the words be few and well chosen. . . . What are the few sentences that will save his soul if I never speak again? . . . Long sermons, weary and injure your usefulness. Be short and sharp; brief, but brimful of the

Gospel."[22] Lacy would make a good seminary instructor with these words.

On the eve of the battle of Chancellorsville, the topic for the *preachers Jackson knew* was, "What is the position of the chaplain in battle, where should he be?" After much discussion, the answer was, "The chaplain should be wherever duty calls him, irrespective." The men of the cloth felt they should never carry a musket, but could assist the ambulance corps, and certainly be available to assist those who were wounded or close to passing into eternity. It was suggested that the chaplains discuss with members of their regiments how the troops felt they could be of most assistance during combat.[23]

It was raining on April 20 in the Fredericksburg area. However, the rain did not dampen the spirits of Thomas J. Jackson. He was expecting company. Around noon a train pulled into Guiney Station. The general could hardly wait until the engine stopped. He leaped from his horse and with the water dripping off his poncho climbed aboard the train. Just a few more feet and he would see the two most important persons in his life, his beloved wife, and his baby daughter Julia. Tom had not seen Anna since she left Winchester in March of '62. And this would be his very first visit with his daughter.

We can almost imagine the moment. After hugging his wife, Tom looked lovingly at little Julia. He did not pick her up though because he was wet. The troops nearby cheered as they rode back to Yerby's. Once they got inside, Tom took his raincoat off. Then he held his precious little daughter, admiring her features, and letting the emotions which he had bottled up for so long go. It was a great moment.

The Jacksons wanted to have Julia baptized during the visit. The uncertainties of war made them realize a long time might pass before they would be together again. The day was set. It was to be private. Tucker Lacy would officiate. However, James P. Smith asked if he might attend. Jackson said "yes." And before long, the staff of the Second Corps, Army of Northern Virginia, was invited. Thus on

April 23 at Yerby's, in the presence of the officers he loved and trusted, Tom and Anna stood before Chaplain Lacy and had little Julia baptized.

Julia was five months old this April day. The rite was held in the parlor of the Yerby home. Tom was even upset because mother and daughter arrived a few moments late. The Yerbys were also present. "The child behaved beautifully, and was the object of great interest to her father's friends and soldiers."

Tucker Lacy also conducted the last church service that Anna and Tom attended together. It was a most memorable day for Anna. It

> . . . being the last upon which I was privileged to attend divine service with my husband on earth, and to worship in camp with such a company of soldiers as I had never seen together in a religious congregation. My husband took me in an ambulance to his headquarters where the services were held, and on the way were seen streams of officers and soldiers, some riding, some walking, all wending their way to the place of worship. Arrived there, we found Mr. Lacy in a tent, in which we were seated, together with General Lee and other distinguished officers. I remember how reverent and impressive was General Lee's bearing, and how handsome he looked. . . . In front of the tent, under the canopy of heaven, were spread out in dense masses the soldiers, sitting upon the benches or standing.[24]

The preaching by Tucker Lacy was earnest and "the singing one grand volume of song." Dr. George Leyburn said the "full and strong voice" of Lacy swept over the crowd. It was a beautiful day. There was standing room only. Jubal Early and J. B. Kershaw were present. "The flower of the Confederate Army was in attendance." Lacy's message was on Lazarus and the rich man, and contrasted this world with the next. They listened with profound attention and respect. Dr. Leyburn wondered how many who were present, like Jackson, were "hearing their last message of heaven."[25]

This was Sunday, April 26. A week later, Tom would be lying in the Wilderness Hospital minus an arm, and two weeks later, he would be gone from this earth. But on this day, he heard Tucker Lacy proclaim the good news of the Gospel.

In a few days, Tucker escorted Mrs. Jackson and Julia to Guiney Station for their departure to Richmond. The Union army was advancing, and Jackson wanted his wife and daughter out of danger.

Lacy baptized Julia on the twenty-third, preached before the general and his wife on April 26, and escorted Mrs. Jackson to the train on the twenty-ninth. Now, however, he had a military task for his commander.

On the morning of the thirtieth, the tents were struck at Yerby's. Aides, teamsters, etc., were very busy. There was a lot of noise and confusion. Jackson returned from a supervisory task, and threw the reins of his horse to his servant Jim and retired into his tent before it was taken down. Jim raised his hand and whispered, "Hush, the General is praying!" Everyone got quiet, and a full quarter of an hour passed before Jackson emerged. His countenance glowed. His last act at Yerby's was devoted to prayer. "With this final preparation he turned to meet the enemies of his country."

On the morning of May 2, Lacy awakened to see Jackson before a campfire. The general knew that Lacy had served in this area and was very familiar with the roads and the terrain. Lacy joined the great commander on the cracker box before the fire. He asked Lacy about the possibility of flanking the Union army, and asked him to mark a map. Tucker was uncertain about Jackson's questions, but stated that the owner of the furnace would surely know. Thus Lacy and Hotchkiss were sent to get exact directions. They were successful. So Lacy aided Jackson in his final military move.

On Sunday morning after Jackson fell at Chancellorsville, Chaplain Lacy went to the tent where Dr. McGuire and Dr. Black had amputated Jackson's arm. Lacy saw the stump where the left arm had been and exclaimed "Oh, General! what a calamity." Jackson thanked him for his kindness and sympathy, but then ministered to the preacher, "You see me severely wounded, but not depressed; not unhappy. I believe that it has been done according to God's holy will, and I will acquiese entirely in it.

157

You may think it strange; but you never saw me more perfectly contented than I am today. . . ."[26]

Jackson went on to say that he felt the wound was in keeping with God's will. Therefore, it was not a calamity, but it would be a great inconvenience. Jackson would be happy to wait until God revealed to him the reason for the event.

He told Lacy that he thought he was going to die on the field, or in the ambulance going to the hospital. However, the general told his preacher friend, "I gave myself up into the hands of my Heavenly Father without a fear." Jackson shared his feelings of peace and victory. "It has been a precious experience to me, that I was brought face to face with death, and found all was well." Jackson's faith did not fail him. He experienced that a child of God can "in the midst of the severest sufferings, fix the thoughts upon God and heavenly things, and derive great comfort and peace. . . ."[27]

Tucker Lacy was so impressed with the faith and words of Jackson that he wrote them down as soon as he left the general's presence and later shared them with R. L. Dabney.

As Lacy was leaving the Wilderness Hospital, he saw Jackson's amputated arm "wrapped up outside" the tent. He picked it up and took it to his brother's place at Ellwood where he buried it. Later Smith placed a marker at the spot, and Jed Hotchkiss buried young Boswell who had gone down with Jackson nearby.

Lacy rode with the general on Monday to Chandler's. After a while, he dismounted from the ambulance and rode on ahead to make preparations for Jackson's arrival at Fairfield. (More about that in the chapter on Smith.)

Once they arrived at Guiney Station, Lacy came as usual at 10:00 a.m. for morning prayers with the general. This he did, May 5-9. On May 7, with Hunter McGuire facing exhaustion, Lacy rode to Hamilton's Crossing to get Dr. Samuel Morrison, Anna's relative.[28]

Mrs. Jackson says that Beverly was "truly a spiritual comforter to me in those dark and agonizing days." When she left Tom's bedside to check on little Julia, she often paused to talk with Lacy, "and bowing down before the throne of grace, pour out our hearts to God to spare that precious, useful life, if consistent with His will. . . ."[29]

Saturday afternoon, the day before his death, despite his breathing problems, Tom called for Lacy and discussed keeping the Sabbath holy.

When Sunday morning came, Lacy wanted to stay by the general's bedside, but Tom insisted that he go and preach to the soldiers. Sandie Pendleton came to his bedside about noon. The general asked, "Who is preaching at headquarters today?" When told it was the Reverend Mr. Lacy and that the whole army was praying for him, he said, "Thank God; they are very kind."[30]

When General Lee saw Lacy coming for the services, he anxiously inquired about Jackson. Lacy said it was hopeless. With deep feeling, Lee exclaimed, "Surely General Jackson must recover. God will not take him from us, now that we need him so much. Surely he will be spared to us, in answer to the many prayers which are offered for him."

His final words to Lacy were, "When you return, I trust you will find him better. When a suitable occasion offers, give him my love, and tell him that I wrestled in prayer for him last night as I never prayed, I believe for myself."

There were many tears shed at the service. The army was melted with grief as they prayed for Jackson. Between twenty-five hundred and three thousand had gathered near Hamilton's Crossing. Lacy preached from Jackson's favorite text, "All things work together for good to them that love God." Romans 8:28. He talked of the comfort that God gives to His children.[31] Many felt that the message helped the men to accept Jackson's fate.

When Lacy returned to Guiney Station, Jackson was gone. He had "passed over the river to rest in the shade of the trees." Lacy spent most of the rest of the day with Mrs. Jackson. She writes:

> Never shall I forget Mr. Lacy's ministrations of consolation to my bleeding heart on that holiest of Sabbath afternoons. Seated by my bedside, he talked so of Heaven, giving such a glowing description of its blessedness, . . . that at last peace, the "peace of God," came into

159

my soul, and I felt that it was selfish to wish to bring back to this sorrowful earth, for my happiness, one who had made such a blissful exchange.[32]

Lacy also rode with Mrs. Jackson in the special car on the funeral train as it headed for Richmond. He did not go to Lexington for the burial, but hastened back to Hamilton's Crossing to attend the seventh meeting of the army chaplains. At noon, William Nelson Pendleton spoke of the duties and responsibilities of a chaplain. He used as his text, I Timothy 2:15, "Study to show thyself approved of God, a workman that needeth not to be ashamed." He urged personal piety.

Beverly Lacy then talked of the death of Jackson, "relating many touching incidents connected with his last moments, and paid a feeling tribute to his memory." Pendleton, a Lexington neighbor of Jackson's, also made comments. The chaplains then united in prayer asking God "that this sad affliction might be sanctified to the good of the army and the country. There was a shadow upon our hearts, for each chaplain felt he had lost his best friend."[33]

Three chaplains, including Lacy, were selected to draw up resolutions "expressive of the feeling of the chaplains of the corps on this sad affliction."

At the next meeting, on May 19, it was reported that Lacy was preaching "to increasing congregations at the old headquarters." Lacy then gave a statement of the closing scenes of General Jackson's life, "which was deeply interesting to all, though it awaked anew the troubled fountains of grief."[34]

Richard S. Ewell was named as successor to Jackson. Lacy accompanied the Second Corps on the march to Pennsylvania, preaching several times during the march and several times each Sunday. He also served with Early in 1864.

Beverly Lacy was a powerful preacher. J. P. Smith says that during one sermon in the spring of 1863, he brought tears to the eyes of both Jackson and Lee. Church leaders felt that he was the right man at the right place. Not only was he accepted in his own denomination, but he had extremely good relations with his colleagues in the Episcopal, Methodist and Baptist ranks.

Even Sandie Pendleton who thought Tucker talked too much, wrote home saying that Tucker had brought new life to the chaplains, had motivated and encouraged them to great zeal. All comments pointed to Lacy being an excellent preacher.

In August of 1863, he preached to fifteen hundred enlisted men, and the officers of the Second Corps. Ewell, Rodes, Early, Johnson, and Ramseur were present. It was a missionary sermon, and one of his best.

On Monday, February 22, 1864, Lacy delivered a two-hour lecture on "The Life and Christian Character of General T. J. Jackson." Again, it was a packed house, and many stood outside, never leaving. "It was a fit and eloquent tribute to a great and good man."[35]

Lacy delivered the message again in April to over three thousand men. Ted Barclay writes, "It was the most attentive audience I ever saw, and how beautifully and touchingly he held up to our view the character of our dearly beloved General as worthy of emulation, especially as Christians."

Lacy was fond of good food, often eating with Dr. Black. When there was a lot to eat and good food, Lacy's prayer of grace was overflowing, but when they had bread, cold pork, and water, it was short, "Lord bless us and save us. Amen."

Dr. Bean, an outstanding history professor of bygone days at Washington and Lee, called Lacy "Stonewall Jackson's Jolly Chaplain." Apparently he was quite a jokester, and told a lot of funny stories. His primary critics seem to have been the Irish Dr. Hunter McGuire of Winchester, and Major Campbell Brown of Early's staff.[36]

After the war, Lacy served as pastor of the Presbyterian Church in Wytheville, Virginia, and at Pine Street Church in Saint Louis. Then he too went into education serving as the agent for the Presbyterian School for Negroes at Tuscaloosa, Alabama. His final church-related job was that of superintendent of the Home Missions of Missouri.

Retiring in 1887, he made his home with his son, John Alexander Lacy, in Washington, D.C. Part of the next thirteen years he was an invalid. But many ministers and scholars came to see him. His granddaughter wrote that when he had visitors, "gales of laughter came from his room."[37]

Death came on November 3, 1900. He was buried in the Jackson Cemetery in Lexington. Dr. J. A. Quarles eulogized him as the "cultured man of letters, the social favorite, . . . the loyal patriot, the eloquent preacher. . . ." This was Beverly T. Lacy, one of the *preachers Jackson knew.*[38]

IX

JAMES POWER SMITH

It was summertime, 1859. Quiet and peace prevailed in the lovely Shenandoah Valley. And at an old brick plantation mansion, called Bellevue, a wedding was taking place. Among the invited guests was a young theological student by the name of James Power Smith. Also attending was Major Thomas J. Jackson, a member of the faculty at Virginia Military Institute and his wife, Mary Anna. To young Smith, Major Jackson looked like a farmer. His wife, though, was "small, . . . very fair, and a most charming and graceful person."[1]

Jackson and Smith were among the last to leave, and it was in this period they met. Jackson mentioned that he had traveled, and Smith, as a minister's son, related a few of his travel experiences. Three years later, the major, by now a general, would send for Smith requesting him to become a member of his staff.

Smith was born at New Athens, Ohio, July 4, 1837, the son of Rev. Joseph Smith and Eliza Bell Smith. His mother was from Winchester, Virginia. Part of James's boyhood was spent in Frederick, Maryland. His father had been a supply pastor there, and then returned during the years 1838 to 1843 as pastor and as headmaster of a school.[2] Junkin, White, Graham, and Smith's father, among the *preachers that Jackson knew,* were connected with schools. That seems to have been the custom in those days. Many schools were operated by churches or by ministers both for Christian education, and also to supplement their salaries.

Young Smith was sent to Jefferson College where he graduated with an A.B. Degree in 1856. Two years later, after teaching awhile himself, James entered Union Theological Seminary, located at the time at Hampden-Sydney.

Spring of 1861 found Smith engaged in his theological studies at Hampden-Sydney in central Virginia. Nearly fifty students were preparing for the ministry under the leadership of men such as R. L. Dabney. However, forces were at work to interrupt their academic career. News of Harpers Ferry and Lincoln's call for troops reached "the remote and peaceful . . . scholastic community."

On the college campus, Dr. Atkinson drilled the students and organized a college company, perhaps much like the Liberty Hall Volunteers. Some of the seminary students, unwilling to make a public display of their feelings, practiced marching in the basement of one of the classrooms.

One day, James found the streets of Farmville filled with people awaiting the arrival of a train from Richmond. Folks on board would bring the news of the legislature and the move toward secession. The local delegate was Attorney Jack Thornton. He addressed the group and said that when Virginia had called for troops during the War for Independence, George Washington had come forth from Westmoreland County to lead the soldiers. Now Westmoreland County had responded again with one of her sons, Robert E. Lee. He would lead "the sons of Virginia in defense of their liberties and their honor."

Like other men in the South, James had to make a decision. He had traveled and lived in the North. His folks were still there. But James was sympathetic to the South, not towards slavery, but he was in favor of States' Rights.

It was a tough choice. To remain in the South would cut him off from his parents. Yet to leave school and to leave Virginia would be deserting his convictions and the cause of the South.

Young Smith went to Richmond to seek the counsel of some friends. He listened to many impassioned speeches about the question of secession from the Union. He was greatly impressed with Henry A. Wise.

164

While he was in Richmond, there came the alarming news that the U.S.S. *Pawnee* was coming up the James River to shell the city "and stop the rebellious movement. The alarm was given just as folks were leaving church. The alarm bell rang from the old arsenal tower in the Capitol Square." Drums rolled. Bugles blew. The Richmond Howitzers responded to the alarm. Fiery speeches filled the air. Women with tears running down their cheeks bade their teenage sons farewell. Old men grabbed flinklock muskets and headed for the banks of the river. The Yankee ship would receive a warm welcome. But the *Pawnee* never came.

Two or three weeks later, Smith was in Winchester, Dr. Graham's town, and a place that would soon become dear to Jackson. The seminary had been closed. All of Smith's belongings were placed in storage in Farmville. They were safe there until Appomattox. At that time, though, Smith's library and the bulk of his prewar possessions disappeared.

Winchester was near the border. Troops from the Shenandoah Valley had already gone to Harpers Ferry. There they were commanded by the officer from VMI whom Smith had met at the wedding two years previously.

One evening as he was riding into town, Smith came upon the leading elements of a marching column. What a sight! It was the Eighth Georgia Infantry headed for Harpers Ferry.

> I had never before seen so large or handsome a military array. There was the band and the flags and the long winding column of soldierly men, with muskets gleaming in the evening sun. At the head, . . . rode the handsome . . . Colonel Francis Bartow. . . . It was an astonishing experience for me to ride beside the colonel, at his request, and guide his fine regiment through the streets of Winchester to a camp in the fields beyond.

A week passed. Smith remained in Winchester and thought, "What shall I do?" Every day more troops arrived in town. He saw young friends and companions in uniforms. The streets of Winchester were decorated with banners.

Five miles away was the bivouac area of the Rockbridge Artillery, commanded by William Nelson Pendleton, a

165

former West Point graduate, and the rector of the Episcopal Church in Lexington. The battery was comprised of college and seminary students, many of the lads planning on entering the ministry. This was just the unit for young Smith.

Amidst tears and concern for his safety, Smith left his friends in Winchester. "I could tarry no longer." Young James donned the Confederate gray, with red artillery cords. A new white haversack hung at his side, filled with food from the lady of the house. In one pocket was a New Testament. In the other, a toothbrush. What more did he need.

His first experience as a soldier was not that pleasant. His skin was still pale. His feet were not tough. He walked alone for five miles. "What a change that hour was making in my life! I was leaving behind so much of books and quiet and peaceful thought. . . ." To make matters worse, at the lane leading to the Rockbridge camp at Stevenson's Depot, he met a carriage filled with pretty young Virginia belles, returning from a visit to the camping area. One of the girls looked at him and said, "Oh, what a clean little soldier." James was hurt.

He was welcomed in camp and taken to meet Captain Pendleton. After a cordial greeting, Smith was assigned to gun number two.

> Thus I, the child of a minister, from a quiet home in a manse, lately out of the cloisters of a divinity school, slight and pale, with no experience of outdoor life and no strength for rude toil and weary march, was a soldier of Confederacy, a private in the artillery of the army of the Valley of Virginia, the proudest earthly distinction that has ever come to me.[3]

It was Smith's feeling that the towns and villages supplied the bulk of the infantry to the Army of Northern Virginia, while the farms and the plantations supplied the riders for the cavalry. These young men were accustomed to the saddle. On the other hand, it seems like most of the artillerymen were students.[4]

The young men from the different background soon became fused and welded "by the overriding conviction of duty and the one compelling passion of patriotic purpose. But in our battery we thought we had the best." This, of course, was the Rockbridge artillery. "At the last, all that were left of the Rockbridge Artillery stood as veteran soldiers beside the guns at Appomattox, and cried like little children at the surrender."[5]

Smith received his basic artillery training north of Winchester. The men were elated at the thought of having fired at Union forces at Falling Waters. They were with Jackson in his baptism of fire on July 2, 1861.

Smith and his mates heard the cheers of the people of Winchester as they left the city on July 18. Jackson read to them the message from General Johnston revealing the urgency of their march to Manassas.

At Millwood "two fair daughters of the Reverend Mr. Peyton Harrison joined their cousins and friends during a break." Three of those present never returned. They fell at Manassas. And before the war was over, Mrs. Peyton and her daughters "had gone to rest beyond the rumors of war and all the pains of separation."

Smith waded the Shenandoah River with the rest of the First Brigade and Jackson. Near the top of Ashby's Gap, an aged black woman brought the hungry soldiers buttermilk and cold hoecakes.

The troops reached Piedmont on the Manassas Gap Railroad and entrained for the east. Friday evening, July 19, "after a long and urgent march, warm, weary, soiled, we found a bivouac in the pines near Mitchell's Ford."[6]

On Sunday, they were ordered into action. "Cannoneers swing to their seats on the limber chests, horses are spurred and lashed into a gallop, officers draw their sabres and shout orders in ringing tones."

A little below the crest of a hill "we dismounted and unlimbered. Before the young divinity student was "the battlefield – lines of blue, with volleys and wreaths of smoke, batteries belching flames – before us. Back of us rode Beauregard and his staff. To and fro passed Jackson, holding up his bandaged hand." The infantry of the First Brigade was on the right and left.

> Our guns were shotted and fired, and it seemed the greatest noise we had ever heard. As I ran from caisson to gun carrying shot, a minie ball flattened itself on the tire of a gun wheel and then struck my right arm, making a bruise like the blow of a stone. With some pride I carried that arm in a sling for a day or two.

After the battle had cooled down, some of the men in Rockbridge Artillery were sent to bring back the guns of the enemy. Smith went to a dying man in blue who struggled to get something from his pocket. It was the picture of a woman and child, the man's family. Smith held it before the poor soul's eyes as they closed in death.

Smith was appalled at the sight of fine horses lying dead in their artillery harness. However, as part of the spoils of war, the harness and guns were added to the Rockbridge Artillery.

That night it rained. It seemed that God was washing the bloody earth. Captured tarpaulin covers were placed over the guns. The men got under the extra covers. "Up at the Henry house the surgeons plied their art, and in the morning beneath the windows the heaps of limbs taken from our wounded men was a picture which the years have not effaced."[7]

Smith then went over to Sudley Church, prisoners were being guarded on the lawn, while the interior of the church was being used as a hospital. In a nearby shop, James met a soldier from New York who had lost both legs, yet he was confident of going home.

The next several months were spent near Centreville. Smith had had a rough introduction to war. In his notes James talks about camp life, the reviews, and Jackson's farewell speech to the First Brigade when he was ordered to Winchester.

Smith has little to say about his military career from that moment until the Maryland campaign.

Smith was with the Army of Northern Virginia when Lee crossed the Potomac at White's Ford. On Sunday, September 7, 1862, he left the camp of the Rockbridge Artillery and rode into Frederick to visit the scenes of his childhood. He met some folks he knew, and was invited to dine in an elegant home. James had a problem though. General Lee was also invited, and young Smith was upset because he had nothing fitting to wear.

During the afternoon he visited the Presbyterian Church on West Second Street. The pastor, the Reverend Mr. Ross, would soon be leaving town. He was in sympathy with the South and the members were not very happy about it. Smith listened to the sermon. At times his eyes and thoughts roamed. He picked out the places where he had sat with his mother, often falling asleep on her lap. He could picture his father standing in the pulpit. When the service was over, he walked through the church of his childhood.

Leaving the church, James was confronted with a sad realization. While he had been at worship, someone had stolen his horse. He went back to camp, and received permission to look for the horse on Monday. No luck.

When he returned, James had another surprise. He was told to report to General Jackson. At first, James thought someone was playing a trick on him. Then Captain Poague confirmed the message.

So young Smith, the son of a minister, and a divinity student at the outbreak of the war, set out to find Jackson's headquarters near Monocacy Junction, three miles south of Frederick. "The general's tents were . . . on a hillside in a grassy field." Jackson was standing in front of the tent, talking to some folks from Frederick. Being shy, Smith stood off to the side. However, Jackson saw him and told him to come forward. The commander and the young student who had met at a wedding three summers earlier, now shook hands.

The general asked James to wait for him in his tent. In a few moments, Jackson entered, and took a seat on a wooden stool he had brought from VMI. Never a person for small talk, Jackson got right to the point, "I have merely sent for you to ask whether you would accept the position of aide-de-camp on my staff." What a surprise, a young artillery corporal being invited to serve on the staff of the war's most famous commander.

After getting over the stunning surprise, Smith offered the excuse that he had no experiences. Jackson was sure that Smith could do the job for him. Just as he had had his eye on Sandie Pendleton, Henry Douglas, and Hunter McGuire, so Jackson saw traits in Smith that were positive.

James still was without a good uniform, and was given permission to ride to Gordonsville where he could obtain the needed clothing.

Returning to camp, Smith found his battery mates very angry. It had been his night to cook, and there was no supper. His friends thought he was making up the story about being invited to Jackson's tent to get off the hook. Again, Captain Poague confirmed the story. This time the men rejoiced at Smith's good fortune, and there was a celebration.

Major John Sherrod of the Thirteenth Virginia came to Smith's aid, giving him some money for a new horse. He bought a young black mare for two hundred dollars in Confederate money. The mare was quite spirited. The first time Jackson and Smith rode together, the mare kicked at Jackson and struck his foot. Jackson never got close again.

James Power Smith missed the Battle of Sharpsburg because he was off to get his new uniform. He rode via Leesburg, Warrenton, and Culpeper. Returning to the army on September 20, he found Jackson camped near Shepherdstown. That night he slept in the general's tent. And the next morning, he rode with Jackson to Lee's headquarters. The famed commander made Smith feel at ease and gave him a fresh peach.

For the next several weeks, the Army of Northern Virginia was encamped in the West Virginia panhandle. Jackson spent almost all of October at Edgewood. This farmhouse was and is still located at Bunker Hill, north of Winchester. Here in this lovely area, a great revival took place. Nightly services were held under the stars of Shenandoah. And as the men saw Jackson walking across the fields to church, they went too. Foreign dignitaries, including a future commander of the British army, came to Bunker Hill to see the famous Jackson.

Jeb Stuart and the cavalry was camped nearby at the

Bower, an estate on a hill overlooking the Opequon Creek. Jeb sent Jackson a new coat, and staff members rode back and forth to visit with each other in spare moments.

During the autumn, Jackson took a day off and went to Winchester to dine at the home of Hunter McGuire, his surgeon. During the meal, McGuire's sister suggested the general get his picture taken. The staff was surprised to see Jackson yield to the request. The result was the famous Winchester photograph, Mrs. Jackson's favorite.

Then it was time to go. Jackson bade fond farewell to his friends, the Grahams. Then he and Smith rode southward. They stopped for a few moments to observe and discuss the battlefield of Kernstown. Then it was on to Middletown, Strasburg, and New Market.

Jackson, Smith, and the others crossed the lovely Massanutten Mountains to the Luray Valley. A few days were spent in the vicinity of Orange Court House. On a cold November day, Jackson, Smith and a few others started for Lee's headquarters at Fredericksburg. By noon, they had reached the home of the Reverend Melzi Chancellor, near Wilderness Church. Snow was falling. It was a bleak day, and the road was full of refugees fleeing from Fredericksburg. "It was a dismal scene." James's future wife, Agnes Lacy, may have been in the group. They also found folks huddled within the walls of Salem Church trying to keep warm. Jackson was visibly touched by the sights.

The horsemen found Lee's headquarters in the pines on the property of Muscoe Garnett. The ground was covered with snow. The air had a bitter chill. After the conference, Jackson and Smith rode to Garnett's house. They were royally welcomed. Jackson slept in bed. James curled up on a rug before the blazing fire. The warmth took the chill from his bones. He thought he was in paradise.

Sunday morning, Jackson and his staff rode into Fredericksburg. The streets were deserted. No church bells were ringing. General Burnside, the new Union commander, was threatening to advance. Barksdale and his men from Mississippi were down by the Rappahannock to turn the move back. Smith says, "We sat in our saddles at the corner of the bank and churches." They looked the situation over and talked. This was Sunday, November 30, 1862. Six years later, James Power Smith became the pastor of the Presbyterian Church that still stands on the corner across from the bank. In 1924, a marker was placed on the corner of the church describing the event.[8]

Lee and Jackson conferred again. Then the staff went to the home of the French family. There they entered into the family devotions. Jackson led the evening prayers, using the big family Bible, and kneeling with the rest for prayer.

Smith was with Jackson as he established headquarters at Chandlers near Guiney Station. The four divisions of the Second Corps were "encamped on the Caroline Hills from Grace Church to Rappahannock Academy and Port Royal. Early on the morning of December 11, Burnside opened with a terrible cannon bombardment on Fredericksburg. The guns wrecked havoc on the city. This was the prelude to the crossing which started on December 12.

To meet this threat, Smith spent most of the day taking messages to the division commanders. They established a strong line of defense on hills overlooking the river. During one of these trips, Smith saw Moss Neck Manor for the first time. It was midnight before he arrived at headquarters near the Hamilton house.

Early in the morning, Smith rode with Jackson to a spot on top of a hill near Telegraph road. There Lee and Jackson conferred and observed the area in their front. The spot is known today as Lee's Hill.

Jackson expected victory. He wore his new coat, a gift from Stuart, and a new hat, purchased for him by Jed Hotchkiss while they were in Martinsburg. He also had a new saber and spurs. He looked so spick-and-span. The soldiers could hardly believe their eyes. The men cheered. The splendor "of their great general was greeted as a good omen on the morn of battle. Everywhere there was confidence, impatient expectation, and the best of spirits."[9]

When the fog lifted about 10:30, Jackson, Smith, and the others saw something that has seldom been seen in America. "The fluttering flags, the long lines of glittering bayonets, the well dressed officers, the prancing horses, the roll of drums, the notes of the bugles. . . ." The Yankees were coming. And Jackson and Longstreet would repulse them. With a strong defensive line, one Union assault after another struck a "Stonewall" and broke. The ground was covered with the bodies of men in blue.

It is not our intention to cover the battle. It was a great victory for Lee. Once again the Union drive to Richmond had been blocked. Jackson was a taskmaster with his officers. He expected the best. When he told a lieutenant to move at 5:00 a.m., he meant exactly that, not 5:01. He was a stickler for detail. As a result, there were often strained relationships. The general and Maxcy Gregg had had their problems, but General Gregg had fallen on the hills of Fredericksburg, turning back the Union assault.

On Saturday evening, December 13, as the Northern Lights were shining in a tremendous display of beauty, Jackson asked Dr. McGuire about the condition of General Gregg. When told that he was fatally wounded, he sent McGuire back to check on the dying officer.

Then, according to Smith, Jackson and the young aide rode to the Yerby house about daylight. Jackson went in to speak with Gregg. The two officers had had their differences, and Gregg, knowing that death was near, wanted to make things right. Jackson said, "The doctors tell me that you have not long to live. Let me ask you to dismiss this matter from your mind and turn your thoughts to God and to the world to which you go." The two shook hands, and tears filled Gregg's eyes. Then Smith and Jackson rode in silence back to a hill near Hamilton's Crossing.

Smith had his memories of the battle. He had ridden across the field of battle to tell Pelham to retire his guns. He also remembered "the fine, handsome blooded mare, the finest animal I ever mounted, that fell under me, cut through by a large piece of shell which sundered the saddle girth under my right foot." Smith lost comrades in the Rockbridge Artillery in the battle too. Jackson wanted to drive the Yankees into the river. It had been a terrible mistake for them.

On the morning of December 15, the Confederates realized the Union army had withdrawn across the Rappahannock. "The heavy mists were slow in rising, but as the sun made its way through, our pickets advanced across the plain and reached the entrenched river road to find that all the proud army of Burnside had gone back to Stafford Heights. . . . Dead bodies were found in piles. . . . Arms and accoutrements, dismounted artillery, and ordnance wagons everywhere strewed the fields."[10]

Confederate leaders thought they might be retreating in an effort to turn the right flank of the Southern lines. Therefore, Lee placed Jackson's command in motion for Caroline Academy and Port Royal.

By late afternoon, Jackson was near Moss Neck church. The question was asked about camp. Someone suggested Moss Neck Manor, the home of the Corbin's. However, Jackson said, "No." So an elegant residence was turned down for a cold night under the stars.

The staff was upset. A halt was called and the men dismounted. Soon a nice fire was made. But there was no food for man nor beast. Jackson asked Smith if he had any biscuits. The answer was negative. The two wrapped themselves together in their overcoats, lying on one blanket, and covering with another. The general got chilled to the bone, and sat up saying he was cold and hungry.

About that time a large dead tree near the fire came crashing down, scattering the embers everywhere, and narrowly missing some of the men. Smith says, "It was a mercy that the Confederate army did not lose its Stonewall by the falling of that tree." The crash must have caused Jackson to make a decision. Smith says Hugh McGuire came and rode to Moss Neck for food. Others say that Pendleton rode to inquire about coming. Anyhow, Jackson said, "Let's go to the 'Moss Neck' house." The early morning hours began a lovely three-month period in the lives of Smith and Jackson.

The Corbin women answered the knocking at the door. Lamps were lighted, "fires stirred and replenished." Jackson went to a bedroom. Smith slept on a nice rug in front of the fire.

Moss Neck was built like a typical English manor house. It was high on a hill with a commanding view. There were extended wings and large porches with fine columns.[11]

Mrs. Richard Corbin offered the general the use of the house, but the commander felt he must share the plight of his troops. With the morning, the wagons came, tents were pitched in the grove beyond the stables, and soon the staff was hard at work.

Two days prior to Christmas, Jackson told Smith he wanted to entertain Lee, Stuart, and Pendleton "at dinner on Christmas day." It was Smith's task to supervise the preparations. He was able to get turkeys, oysters, a ham, cake, and a bottle of wine, biscuits, and pickles.

It was a great occasion, and one of the most memorable for the officers of the Army of Northern Virginia. It was also Jackson's last Christmas, and one that Smith never forgot. After the military dinner, Mrs. Corbin had an old-fashioned party for the younger members of the staff. Smith, Pendleton, and others were very much impressed with lovely Kate Corbin. As time passed, Sandie Pendleton won her hand. And one of the pleasures of the winter was that of Jackson watching his young officer falling in love.

Jackson caught cold, and Dr. McGuire persuaded the general to occupy a small frame house which had been used as an office.

Smith describes Jackson's office at Moss Neck:

> [It] was a small frame house, a story and a half high, which stood to the left and front of the mansion, under the pine trees. It was a country gentlemen's office. There was a little lobby in the front; on the left a wood closet, and on the right a narrow stair way leading to an attic room. An open fireplace was at the opposite end from the door. On either side of the door were bookshelves, on which stood farmer's books, horse and cattle registers, agricultural reports, Virginia codes, and a . . . lot of old time volumes. On the walls hung framed pictures of famous horses and fine cattle. . . . The general's cot was placed on one side, and a small table on the other. Two or three stools completed the furniture. On the wall hung the general's sword, his overcoat and cap, and in the corner lay his boots. A guard marched to and fro before the door. . . .

175

In the morning the members of the staff, one after another called with reports of conditions and wants: quartermaster, commissary, ordnance, medical affairs all passed daily under his attention and necessary orders were issued or communications written.[12]

Jackson and his staff are gone now. But "Moss Neck is still standing and standing majestically," a lovely antebellum Virginia house. The house is part of a fifteen-hundred-acre estate owned by folks connected with Sears. Jackson's office, however, is gone.

In the "evening dews and damps" one can picture couriers coming and going, Jackson planning, and discussions with Pendleton, McGuire, Hawks, and James Smith.

During this winter, Jackson brought in Col. Charles Faulkner to work on reports of his previous actions. Jed Hotchkiss did the accompanying maps. Mornings were spent on administrative detail. In the afternoon, Jackson took a ride to look at troop encampments and positions or took a long walk. The evenings were spent working on reports or in staff discussions.

Jackson was appalled at the suffering of Fredericksburg, and issued an appeal to the officers and men of his command for their relief. Thirty thousand dollars was raised.

An old drawing of the Presbyterian Church, Fredericksburg.

Jackson contributed one hundred dollars himself. Smith served as the treasurer of this fund.

At daybreak of April 29, "sleeping in our tents at corps headquarters, near Hamilton's Crossing, we were aroused by Major Samuel Hale of Early's staff, with the stirring news that Federal troops were crossing the Rappahannock under cover of a heavy fog."[13]

A messenger was sent to Yerby's to inform General Jackson. The news brought him his last moments with Anna and Julia. He immediately ordered his division commanders to prepare for action.

Smith was sent across the fields to tell General Lee. The Confederate leader was still asleep. However, Colonel Venable on his staff told Smith to go in and break the news. Then it was back to Jackson. Smith was then dispatched to Yerby's with the news that the general would be unable to return. Mrs. Jackson was to leave the area as battle was pending. This was the beginning of Jackson's final days.

Throughout the twenty-ninth and thirtieth, the Confederates in positions held during the previous December, watched and waited Union developments. Part of the Second Corps was moved on the thirtieth toward Chancellorsville. Cheers rolled along the line when Lee and Jackson rode by.

Smith describes the encampment of Lee and Jackson on this historic night, at the point where the road turned left toward the old Catherine Furnace. They rested on pine straw, "curtained only by the close shadow of the pine forest." Smith was sent on an errand by General Lee. When he returned, Lee was sleeping at the foot of a tree, "covered with his army cloak." He pulled Smith under the cloak and asked him to give his report.

Smith then went off to make his own bed, "with my head in my saddle, near my horse's feet, [I] was soon wrapped in the heavy slumber of a wearied soldier."

Young J.P. then became an eyewitness to one of the great moments in American History.

Sometime after midnight I was awakened by the chill of the early morning hours, and turning over, caught a glimpse of a little flame on

177

the slope above me, and sitting up to see what it meant I saw, bending over a scant fire of twigs, two men seated on old cracker boxes and warming their hands over the little fire. I had to rub my eyes and collect my wits to recognize the figures of Robert E. Lee and Stonewall Jackson. Who can tell the story of that quiet council of war between two sleeping armies?[14]

Apparently this was the time, during the cracker box conference, that the famous flank march was planned. When daylight came, Smith was awakened with the news, "Get up, Smith, the general wants you."

In a moment I was mounted and at the side of the general, who sat on his horse by the roadside, as the long line of our troops cheerily, but in silence as directed, poured down the Furnace road. His cap was pulled low over his eye, and looking up from under the visor, with lips compressed, . . . he nodded to me, and in brief and rapid utterance, . . . he gave me orders for our wagon and ambulance trains.

All was in motion for one of Lee and Jackson's greatest movements. About 3:00 p.m., Smith found Jackson, seated on a stump by the Brock Road writing a dispatch to Lee:

General. The enemy has made a stand at Chancellor's, which is about two miles from Chancellorsville. I hope so soon as practicable to attack.

I trust that an ever kind Providence will bless us with success.

Jackson then rode forward with Fitz Lee to scout the position of Howard's Union Eleventh Corps. His friend, General Paxton, commanding the Stonewall brigade, was sent to hold the junction of the Germanna Plank Road and the Orange Road.

Robert Rodes was leading the advance of the Second Corps. Victory and disaster were just hours away. It would have been a great movie script.

"Are you ready, General Rodes?" asked Jackson.

"Yes, sir," replied Rodes.

"You can go forward then," said Jackson.

Rodes nodded. A bugle blew, followed by many others. Then the long gray lines swept forward through the brush and woods. Rebel yells filled the air, reaching all the way to Hooker's headquarters at Chancellorsville. What a moment! One of the finest in the career of General T. J. Jackson, and in the history of the Second Corps. The gray line swept forward and overran the camp of the Eleventh Corps.

By 8:00 p.m. twilight was falling. Smith gathered his couriers to find Jackson. Riding east, James reached a point a mile west of Chancellorsville. He saw Robert Rodes and was told that Jackson was just ahead.

James rode forward about one hundred yards, and heard shooting. Momentarily he met Captain Taylor of Hill's staff who stated that Jackson and Hill had been wounded and many around them killed by the fire of their own men. The distressed Smith spurred his horse and rode to find Jackson.

Jackson had been checking troop alignments when other men in gray, unaware of his presence, opened fire. Smith's friend, James K. Boswell, fell from the saddle, dead. Jackson was met with a second volley from Pender's men. "He was struck by three balls at the same time. One went through the palm of his right hand; a second passed through the wrist of the left arm and out the hand. The third one was more severe. It passed through the left arm half-way from the shoulder to the elbow. The large bone of the upper arm was splintered to the elbow joint, and the wound bled freely."

His horse turned from the fire, and dashed through thick bushes. Jackson's cap was pulled off, and his forehead scratched. Drops of blood fell on his face. He lost control of the reins and reeled from the saddle. Captain Wilbourn caught him and placed him gently on the ground. A. P. Hill came to his aid.

It was at this moment, that J. P. Smith arrived. He cut the coat sleeve open from the wrist to the shoulder, and used his handkerchief to stem the flow of blood. Couriers were sent to find Dr. Hunter McGuire, and to obtain an ambulance.

Realizing that Jackson needed to be moved, a group of litter bearers were assembled. Smith carried one corner. One of the team was struck by a shot and fell. Major Leigh of Hill's staff kept the litter from falling.

179

Smith's letter concerning Jackson. Courtesy the National Park Service

The fire became heavier. The bearers panicked. The stretcher was placed in the middle of the road, with Smith shielding Jackson's body with his own. When the firing slackened, young Smith helped Jackson up, put his arms around him, and started to drag him to safety. More litter bearers arrived. Again they started to carry him to safety. Another bearer fell. This time Jackson fell and hit the ground. The fall caused him great pain.

Finally, after great effort, they were able to reach a point of comparative safety. The general was placed in an ambulance. At Chancellor's Dr. McGuire met them and took

James Power Smith. Courtesy the Presbyterian Historical Foundation

charge. "Through the night, back over the battlefield of the afternoon, we reached the Wilderness store, and in a field on the north the field hospital of our corps. . . . Here we found a tent prepared, and after midnight the left arm was amputated near the shoulder, and a ball taken from the right hand." Smith held the light for the operation. And "all night long it was mine to watch by the sufferer and keep him warmly wrapped and undisturbed in his sleep."[15]

Jackson came out from under the anesthetic rather

quickly. James Smith, who had held the lights during the operation, helped the general drink a cup of coffee.

Shortly after 3:00 a.m., Dr. McGuire entered the tent with a visitor. It was Sandie Pendleton. He had gone for McGuire when he heard the news that Jackson had fallen, and then fainted himself. However, Sandie had to keep on going carrying messages. Now about the fourth watch of the night, he came with a question from Jeb Stuart.

Jackson recognized him, and spoke with a strong voice, "Well, Major, I am glad to see you; I thought you were killed." Sandie breathed a sigh of relief, and his heart filled with hope for his friend's recovery. Briefly Pendleton sketched the events of the last several hours. Now he came from Stuart to see if Jackson had any orders.

Jackson asked some crucial questions. He paused for a moment, and then replied that Stuart who was on the scene should do as he thought best.

After Sandie left, Jackson stayed awake and talked with Smith. He stated that chloroform was a good invention, but he would not like to meet death while under its influence. The vapor took away pain, but he could remember a faint sound like delightful music. "I believe it was the sawing of the bone." Finally McGuire insisted that Jackson get some sleep. Smith concurred.

The sun had risen by the time Jackson awoke at 9:00 a.m. He had little pain, looked bright, and took some food. He listened to the guns of battle booming in the east. The sounds were fading away. No doubt Stuart was chasing them. That was good, very good. All of this made McGuire feel optimistic.

Once again we see Jackson's physical strength. Despite being hit three times, being placed by the roadside once, falling from a litter once, dragged for a distance by Smith, and then enduring a ride in an army ambulance, going through shock, and having an amputation, he was very alert. His mind rose to the occasion. All the staff but James Smith must resume their duties. Stuart needed the benefit of their wisdom. The enemy must be pressed, and Stuart given all the assistance possible. Joseph Morrison must ride to Richmond and tell Anna what had occurred. If possible, he wished her brought to him.

Later in the morning he experienced some discomfort. However, he was glad to see Chaplain Lacy. The minister exclaimed, "Oh, General! What a calamity." Jackson almost preached to Lacy, saying the Lord would reveal to him in the afterlife the reason for the loss of his arm. The general said he felt great peace as he was being brought to the field hospital. He thought he was dying, but there was no fear, only peace.

Henry Kyd Douglas arrived but did not get to see Jackson. He brought the news that Boswell had been killed. Hotchkiss had found his body and buried him at Ellwood. Henry also brought the sad news that Frank Paxton, Jackson's Lexington friend, neighbor and fellow Presbyterian, had been killed. The good news was that the Stonewall brigade had made a splendid charge. Stuart had made an emotional appeal, and the First Brigade responded in a magnificent manner. This news brought tears to Jackson's eyes.

Things grew quiet. Afternoon came and a courier galloped up from General Lee's headquarters. James P. Smith took the message and gave it to Jackson. Robert E. Lee said, "Could I have directed events, I should have chosen for the good of the country to be disabled in your stead. I congratulate you upon the victory, which is due to your skill and energy."

Jackson looked away, deeply touched and moved. He would have been affected even more had he known that Lee's voice choked with emotion as he dictated the note.

Guiney Station

Robert E. Lee felt it would be best to move Jackson to a safer spot. The Yankees could launch a counterattack and overrun the area of the Wilderness Hospital. Jackson was not afraid. He had always been very humane with the Federal wounded, and he was sure they would treat him courteously. Hunter McGuire, Jacksons' surgeon, was ordered to accompany the fallen commander.

Stonewall was asked if he had a preference, or a choice

183

of a recovery site. He remembered the kindness of the Chandler's at Guiney Station. It was a good place, and close to the railroad. The train could take him to Richmond in an emergency, or transfer him there later.

Early on Monday morning, May 4, he was tenderly placed in an army ambulance. The driver slapped the reins and the twenty-five-mile trip to Thomas Coleman Chandler's Fairfield plantation was begun. The route was via the Brock Road to Spotsylvania Court House, thence to Massaponax Church and Guiney Station. Jed Hotchkiss and a small group of pioneers rode ahead to clear the road.

In the ambulance with General Jackson were Dr. Hunter McGuire, Chaplain Beverly T. Lacy, and James Power Smith. Another aide, Joseph Morrison, had been sent to Richmond to tell his sister Anna about the wounding of her husband.

It was a long trip. The news had spread. Along the route, Virginians gathered to watch the ambulance pass by, and to make encouraging remarks. A large crowd gathered as the ambulance stopped for water at the well at Spotsylvania Court House.

Noon came. The children played in the spacious yard at Fairfield. Mrs. Chandler and the others were busy at their tasks. Some wounded Confederates were being treated in the big house. Across the yard, the big office stood empty, with the exception of some items that had been stored. It almost seemed haunted. Soon, however, it would be a busy place.

A courier rode up to tell Mrs. Chandler the ambulance was approaching. Mammy Phyliss and Aunt Judy, two of Mrs. Chandler's servants, prepared a bed in the parlor for the wounded hero of the Confederacy.

Chaplain Lacy arrived before the ambulance. He felt the mansion house was too crowded and offered too little privacy. Hunter McGuire rode up and concurred with Lacy. The chaplain looked around, and then saw the little office. "Why not use the little house out in the yard?" Mrs. Chandler said, "Fine." A historic decision was made.

There was little time now. A storm was brewing. The servants hurriedly swept and cleaned the former office, and aired it out. A fire was made in the big stone fireplace. Hopefully, this would be the building from which General Jackson would recover and go forth to lead his army to more victories.

Tom Chandler stood by the gate to meet the ambulance as it drew up. The general was removed on a stretcher, and apologized for being unable to shake hands. The right hand was bandaged from the lesser wound. Jackson was placed in one room, the adjoining room was to be used as a waiting room, and as Dr. McGuire's office. A mantel clock was placed in Jackson's room.

Jackson had withstood the trip well. He chatted a lot along the route, talking about Hooker's plans, and the Stonewall brigade. His mind was very clear. It was almost 8:00 p.m. when he reached Fairfield. He was tired and slept well.

Things looked good on Tuesday, May 5. McGuire changed bandages, and was pleased with the way the amputation was healing. A lounge and chairs were added by Mrs. Chandler to make things more comfortable. Jackson ate breakfast, and Chaplain Lacy led morning prayers. The general said, "You must come every morning." Jed Hotchkiss returned to duty. Young James Power Smith remained at Guiney Station with the general and Dr. McGuire. The next day the two Presbyterians discussed theological matters.

And on this Wednesday, Chaplain Lacy went to see General Lee. He reported on Jackson's progress at Fairfield, and requested the services of Dr. Samuel B. Morrison, the general's family doctor, and Anna's. Morrison's presence would permit Hunter McGuire to get some rest. Lee also sent a message with the chaplain, "Tell him [Jackson] to make haste and get well, and come back to me as soon as he can. He has lost his left arm; but I have lost my right arm."

Wednesday night, McGuire was exhausted. He could stay awake no longer. He instructed Jim to keep watch, and he stretched out on the lounge in Jackson's room. Toward morning, the general became nauseated. Not wanting to waken McGuire, Jackson told Jim to place a wet towel on his stomach. Jim reluctantly obeyed. But it did not help. The pain got worse, and at dawn he asked Jim to waken McGuire.

The doctor from Winchester was alarmed. He recognized the early symptoms of pneumonia. While McGuire was dressing the general's wounds, Anna, her brother Joseph, Nurse Hetty, and baby Julia arrived. Anna sensed there was trouble. Mrs. Chandler tried to reassure her, taking her to quarters in the big house. Anna saw a bad omen though. In the yard the body of General Frank Paxton, a Lexington friend and neighbor, was being removed from a temporary grave. It was a chilling moment. Fear gripped her heart.

She composed herself the best she could and went in to see her husband. What a difference. Two weeks ago in Yerby's all had been so well, they were so happy. At the baptism of Julia and at church with her Tom, she was on top of the world. Now her world had fallen apart, and things looked bad. She thought of Paxton's widow, and shuddered "under the weight of apprehension and horror." Tom told her to cheer up, and stated that God knew what was best for them.

Then Jackson drifted off. The medicine and the pain were too much. He issued orders and talked of battle. Mrs. Hoge came from Richmond to stand with Anna. Friday and Saturday were much like Thursday. Breathing was difficult, but he still wanted to talk with Chaplain Lacy on Saturday afternoon. In the evening, he asked Anna to sing for him, the most spiritual songs possible. It was difficult, but she did as he wished, closing at his request with Psalm 51 in verse.

Early on Sunday morning, Dr. Morrison told his relatives that the end was near. They had done all they could, but it was not enough. Life was ebbing away. Anna knew she had to tell him so he could make his final spiritual preparation. With a prayer for composure and guidance she went in to tell him the news. He showed no surprise or concern,

186

but seemed to rejoice in the certainty of seeing his Redeemer face to face.

He responded in the affirmative when Anna asked him if he wished her to return to her family's home in North Carolina with little Julia, and said that he wanted to be buried in "Lexington, in my own plot."

Mrs. Hoge brought Julia in. His face brightened, he smiled and said, "Little darling! Sweet one!" Tears filled the room. Emotions could not be controlled.

He asked Sandie Pendleton, who was almost an adopted son, who was preaching at headquarters. Sandie replied, "Mr. Lacy. The whole army is praying for you."

Weakly, the general said, "They are very kind. It is the Lord's Day. My wish is fulfilled. I have always desired to die on Sunday."

On the mantel, Mrs. Chandler's clock ticked away. It struck two o'clock, then three. Fifteen minutes later, Thomas Jonathan Jackson "crossed over the river to rest under the shade of the trees."

The Reverend Mr. Lacy shared with Anna the glories of heaven and comforted her. His body was carefully prepared by "the loving hands of the staff officers, the body being embalmed and clothed in ordinary dress, and then wrapped in the dark-blue military overcoat." His Confederate uniform had been cut almost to pieces by his attendants, in their endeavor to reach and bind up his wounds on the night of his fall.

Sunday, April 26, Anna had spent the day with her husband. Together they had gone to church with General Lee and many others. Now just fourteen days later she was a widow. Her husband had died at Guiney Station. She was alone to face life with her infant daughter.

Sunday evening, just two weeks ago, she had walked in the evening with her husband. This Sunday evening Anna took another walk. This time to the Chandler mansion, to the parlor. Her husband was asleep, asleep in death. She gazed upon

    . . . all that was left of the one who had been to me the truest, tenderest, and dearest of all relations of earth – the husband of whom I had been so proud, and for who I thought no honors or distinctions too great; but above all this I prized and revered his . . . Christian character, and I knew that God had now given him a "crown of righteousness."[16]

Her Tom was dead before he was forty, dead in the prime of life. "But 'alive in Christ,' for evermore."

Hours later, Anna dozed off in exhaustion, but then awakened. It was still. A full moon flooded the room. It was lovely, but her heart was broken, full of anguish and grief. At the midnight hour, with little Julia and Mrs. Hoge sleeping nearby, Mary Anna Jackson faced the "terrible reality of my loss and the desolation of widowhood."

This was Sunday, May 10, 1863, at Guiney Station, Virginia. Mighty Stonewall was dead. A widow mourned. Young staff officers cried, and the Confederacy was filled with grief.

The Capitol

Monday morning, May 11, Mrs. Jackson went once again to the Chandler parlor to view the remains of the man they called Stonewall. To the Confederacy, he was their hero. But he was her husband. The casket was covered with the flowers of spring. "His dear face was wreathed with the lovely lily of the valley."[17]

His body was carried to the train, and the sad journey to Richmond began. A special car was set apart for Mrs. Jackson. The Reverend Mr. Lacy and the staff officers, Jed Hotchkiss, Henry Douglas, Sandie Pendleton, Hunter McGuire, and James Smith were also in the car.

When the funeral train reached the suburbs of Richmond, it stopped. Carriages sent by Governor Letcher met them and took the folks to the governor's mansion.

Business stopped, and people thronged the streets to pay tribute to the funeral cortege. There were the dirges of the military band, and the booming of the cannon. Eyes filled with tears. It was one of the saddest days in the history of Richmond.

The casket covered with the Confederate flag was placed in "the centre of the reception room in the Executive Mansion." It was there that Anna Jackson looked upon the face of her husband for the last time.

On Tuesday, a great military and civic procession took place. The body was carried through the main streets of the city. The pallbearers were general officers. The hearse was draped in mourning and pulled by four white horses. Little Sorrel followed the hearse. Next came the members of his staff, marching for the last time behind their friend and leader.

Following the staff came military units, and the president, cabinet, and other dignitaries.

> Every place of business was closed, and every avenue thronged with solemn and tearful spectators, while a silence more impressive than the Sabbath brooded over the whole town. When the hearse reached the steps of the Capitol, the pall bearers, headed by General Longstreet, . . . bore the corpse into the lower house of the Congress, where . . . it was placed . . . before the speaker's chair. The coffin still . . . enfolded with the white, blue, and red of the Confederate flag.

A new design had been made for a flag. The first model had just been completed. The plan was for it to fly over the capitol. However, President Davis sent the flag "as a gift of the country, to be the winding sheet of General Jackson."

Throughout the day the body lay in state. Over twenty thousand persons came to pay their respects. Flowers covered the casket, the speaker's chair, and others were piled around the room.

An old soldier who had given his arm for his country came just as the gates were being closed. He was told that he was too late, but made an impassioned plea to "see my general once more." Governor Letcher yielded to his request. The old soldier went in and wept over the casket.

Mrs. Jackson remained secluded nearby. A few friends came to share her tears, and Rev. Dr. T. V. Moore shared with her the precious words of John 14: "Let not your heart be troubled, . . . in my Father's house are many mansions . . .. I go to prepare a place for you." In her sorrow, Anna took comfort in the fact that her Tom had stepped through the door to a room prepared for him in the Father's house.

189

Home at Last

Wednesday morning, May 13, the casket was taken to the train for the trip to Lexington. The route was via Gordonsville to Lynchburg. People lined the tracks, and at every station where a stop was made, saddened Virginians handed floral arrangements to those on board. People asked to see little Julia.

At Lynchburg, the group transferred from the train to a canal boat for the last leg of the journey. On Thursday evening, May 14, "we reached the little village which had been so dear to him, and where his body was now to repose."

"Dr. White and our friends met us in tears and sorrow." The body was placed under the charge of the cadets of Virginia Military Institute. Jackson was returned to the lecture room where he had taught for ten years. Cadets stood guard throughout the night.

The last scene in the Jackson tragedy occurred on Friday, May 15, 1863. Jackson's body was escorted from the lecture hall at Virginia Military Institute to the Presbyterian Church. Dr. White, Jackson's "spiritual commander," presided. The service was kept plain and dignified in accordance with the devotion and simplicity of the general's life.

Dr. Ramsey of Lynchburg offered prayer. Then the hymn, "How Blest the Righteous When He Dies," was sung. Dr. White read 1 Corinthians 15. The scripture lesson was followed by a brief message.

The service was over. Now came the trip to the cemetery. It still seemed like a dream. Anna, the staff, soldiers, cadets, friends and neighbors followed the casket.

"The spot where he rests is beautiful for situation – the gentle eminence commanding the loveliest views of peaceful, picturesque valleys, beyond which, like faithful sentennials, rise the everlasting hills."

Thomas Jonathan Jackson left Virginia Military Institute as an obscure teacher in April of 1861. Now he was back in Lexington, "home at last."

Years later, Dr. Harry J. Warthen was present in Sunday School classes taught by Dr. Smith in Richmond. The students knew they could get the cleric sidetracked by asking questions about Jackson. One day Warthen asked Smith, "Why did a just God permit a man so good and so badly needed to be killed at such a critical time."

Smith had a reply: "When the Lord in His infinite wisdom, decided it was best for the South to lose, He realized it was necessary to dispose of His servant Stonewall first." This ties in with Jackson's explanation of why Napoleon lost at Waterloo. It was best in God's plan and design.

The staff assigned Smith the task of going with Mrs. Jackson and little Julia to the Morrison home in North Carolina. When he returned to Richmond, there was a letter from Gen. R. S. Ewell, inviting him to become a member of his staff. Smith proceeded to Winchester and followed the army north.

He crossed the Potomac on June 29 at Williamsport. At sunset he reached Greencastle, Pennsylvania. A lot of folks were gathered in the streets talking about the invasion. Young J.P. expected trouble, and kept his hand on his pistol.

Chambersburg was reached by dawn on Tuesday, June 30. He found General Lee in Messerschmidt's woods east of town. "Lee was about to mount with his staff, when he saw me and called me to him. After giving me a kind greeting, and hearing of my all night ride, he inquired with much tenderness of Mrs. Jackson and her child and then spoke with sadness and emotion of the loss he had experienced in the death of Jackson."[18]

Lee then asked if he knew anything about Jeb Stuart. Smith said he had ridden part way with two couriers. Lee expressed surprise. He had expected Stuart to report to him in Pennsylvania. "Lee was troubled that his cavalry forces were not between him and the enemy, as he had expected them to be."

By Lee's request, Smith remained with the commander throughout the thirtieth and that night, Smith was with the general when he first heard the sound of the guns on July 1 at Gettysburg. "I recall that it was a surprise and something spoken of with regret that an engagement had been brought on."

191

Smith left Lee on the hills west of the battlefield and rode across country to find Ewell. "I was cordially greeted by him and his party, and I rode with them into the town behind our advancing lines."[19]

Ewell reined up at the square in Gettysburg, remaining there for some time, sending and receiving couriers, making troop dispositions, and directing supplies, and the rearward movement of Union prisoners.

Jubal Early and Robert Rodes came in from the front, very much excited about their prospects and advanced to the slopes of Cemetery Hill. They conveyed to Ewell their "earnest desire to advance upon the cemetery hill in front of the town, provided they were supported by troops on the right."

Ewell, knowing that Smith had just come from Lee, requested James to find him, and report the wishes of Rodes and Early. James talked a few moments, and then rode back toward the seminary. Soon he found Lee and Longstreet and conveyed the message sent by Rodes and Early. It was now about 5:00 p.m.

Lee pointed to the higher ground, and noted the Yankees in possession of Cemetery Hill. Lee then said, "Our people are not all up yet, and I have no troops with which to occupy this higher ground." He then turned and asked Longstreet how far his divisions were from Gettysburg. When told they "were on the road from Chambersburg, and still quite a distance," Lee seemed disappointed. Longstreet's answer was indefinite and conveyed no zeal to move his men forward with great haste. Smith was the only one present. And the young theologian must have lamented the loss of his friend Jackson, who certainly would have pressed on to Cemetery Hill.

With this sad experience, both for Smith and the Confederacy, we leave the war period, and pick up the life of James P. Smith at the conclusion of hostilities.

When the war ended, Smith went back to seminary. He graduated from Union and on October 13, 1866, was ordained by the Montgomery Presbytery. He assumed the pastorate of a Presbyterian church in Roanoke, and was serving there when the call came from Fredericksburg.

The date was April 13, 1869, the Session voted to invite Smith, "in charge at Big Lick, Roanoke County" (now known as Roanoke) to visit the church and preach a trial sermon. James accepted the invitation. His trial sermon was very impressive, and the Fredericksburg Church voted on May 24, 1869, "to seek permission from the Presbytery to call him."

After all the church formalities were taken care of, Smith arrived in Fredericksburg and was installed on the second Sunday in November 1869. Dr. Moses D. Hoge preached the sermon and delivered the charge. That Sunday afternoon began an association that was to last for twenty-three years.

Not only was Smith active in building up the church, but also in stressing the heritage of the Confederacy. He shared in the dedication of the Jackson Monument in Richmond, and at the Memorial Hall in Lexington, and offered prayers at the dedication of the monument to Hunter Holmes McGuire in Richmond. Nearer home, he took the lead in erecting monuments at places connected with the life of Jackson. Among these were the spot on the Lacy farm were Jackson's arm was buried, and a marker on the wall of the church depicting Jackson stopping on the cold November Sunday.

Smith had accompanied Jackson's body to Lexington. In the years that followed, he conducted, or shared in funeral services for many who had been officers or enlisted men in the ranks of the Confederacy. Naturally, he shared in the service for Dr. McGuire.

On the north bank of the Rappahannock River, situated between present-day U.S. 1 and U.S. 3, is Chatham, a lovely colonial estate, and one of the most historic homes in America. The large brick house was begun in 1768 by William Fitzhugh, a young Virginian of great wealth. It was named after William Pitt, the Earl of Chatham.

Many distinguished Americans have come to Chatham. George Washington was one of them. A friend of Fitzhugh, George was a frequent visitor, and he brought his bride,

Martha Custis here on their way north to Mount Vernon. It seems like he spent his honeymoon at Chatham.

The Civil War and "the tragic era" brought an end to the plantation type existence of Chatham. When the war broke out, the estate was owned by the Lacy family. We have already met them. Major J. Horace Lacy, Beverly's brother, owned Chatham, and Ellwood, 15 miles west of Fredericksburg. Winters were spent at Chatham, while summers were spent west of town.

Sadly, both places stood in the advance of the Union army. In the spring of 1862, another great American came to Chatham. This time it was none other than the president of the United States. Mr. Lincoln came to discuss strategy with General McDowell who was cooperating in the latest on to Richmond movement.

After Antietam, Union forces, this time under General Burnside, occupied the north bank of the river. Men in blue were all over the estate. General Edwin Sumner used Chatham as his headquarters while preparing to attack Lee. Pontoons were placed across the river just under the brow of the hill. And in the exchange of cannon fire, Lee used his field glasses to see if the tree under which he had courted his wife at Chatham was still standing. Clara Barton and Walt Whitman came to Chatham to nurse the wounded after the battle.

The soldiers ripped paneling from the walls and used it to make firewood. They also wrote their names on the walls, and left things in a poor state of repair.

Ellwood, near the junction of the Orange and Culpeper roads and the bridge over Wilderness Run, was built in 1774 by William Jones. This place also hosted famous visitors, including Lafayette, James Madison, and Light Horse Harry Lee.

Jones's second wife was the mother of Betty Churchill Jones. Betty, who was born on June 21, 1829, married James Horace Lacy on October 14, 1848. Mrs. Lacy inherited both Chatham and Ellwood.

Mrs. Lacy and her children fled from the advance of the Union armies in 1862. James P. Smith may have met them at Salem Church, or on the road westward in late November. Smith was near Ellwood in May of 1863. There near the main house, Lacy buried the amputated arm of General Jackson, and later Smith erected a marker.

After the war, the Lacys picked up the pieces and started to restore Chatham. And it was here that James P. Smith courted the daughter of Horace and Betty Lacy. On April 26, 1871, Agnes and James were married at the historic estate overlooking the Rappahannock.

Today, thanks to John Pratt and the National Park Service, one can step back into history, and walk where George Washington, Robert E. Lee, Abraham Lincoln, Ambrose Burnside, Edwin Sumner, Clara Barton, Walt Whitman, Mark Sullivan, and a whole host of ordinary folks have walked.

We can envision climbing the hill in a carriage and looking at plantation life, or close our eyes and see the fields filled with soldiers, campfires, horses, and cannon.

And we can walk to the hill in front of Chatham, and see historic Fredericksburg from the same view as the Union commanders and previous owners.

Or one can walk down to the Rappahannock and imagine that he was a Union soldier preparing to cross the river in 1862. Or just maybe we can imagine the young theologian James Smith courting Miss Agnes, and maybe we can picture their wedding in the spring of 1871.

This is Chatham, the home of Horace Lacy, and the place where James Power Smith did his courting.

James Power Smith spent twenty-three years as pastor of the Fredericksburg Presbyterian Church. He was known and loved in the church and community.[20] However, he made a very unique contribution to the Presbyterian Church in Virginia. He was the only man in the history of the Synod of Virginia to serve "fifty years in succession as its stated clerk." The half century period was from 1870 to 1920. Young and old alike looked to him for advice, wisdom, and leadership.

When he left Fredericksburg he did evangelistic work for one year in the Charlottesville area. Then he became editor and owner of the *Central Presbyterian,* a leading church periodical of its day. In 1893 Dr. Smith moved to Richmond. In "the first city of the Confederacy" he edited his periodical for eighteen years.

His Sunday mornings, being free, he was in great demand for special services. Often he spoke for services where comrades of his days with Jackson were either members of, or pastor of the church.

Much time was spent in visiting the Soldiers Home, sharing his time with the veterans, and preaching for them. From time to time he dropped into the office of Hunter Holmes McGuire, Jackson's doctor, and another member of the staff.

Once a month, Dr. Smith held services at the state prison. When he was free, or if he was in town, he went to the eleven o'clock service at Second Presbyterian where Dr. Hoge was the pastor.

In addition to all of this, he was chairman of the committee dealing with Presbyterian Sunday School and Christian education materials. Other duties included chaplain of the First Battalion, Virginia Artillery, in the National Guard, "Past Commander and Chaplain of the R. E. Lee Camp of the Confederate Veterans, Director of the Mary Washington Association in Fredericksburg, and writer of many church and historical articles."

Smith wrote many reports and notes for Jackson. Naturally, this carried over into the postwar years as he wrote his sermons. And Smith wrote of many of his wartime experiences in *Battles and Leaders of the Civil War, The Southern Historical Society Papers,* and in the *Central Presbyterian.*

Smith made another trip to Gettysburg. The date was June 9, 1917. The occasion, the dedication of the Virginia State monument on Seminary Ridge. An article from the time reads:

> The Invocation was pronounced by Rev. James Power Smith, captain and aide-de-camp on staff of Gen. Thos. J. Jackson, Army of Northern Virginia.

The *Richmond Times Dispatch* notes that Governor Henry Carter Stuart delivered the address and presented the Vir-

The J. P. Smith family.

ginia memorial to the nation. Trains brought members of
the blue and gray to the battlefield once again. They had a
reunion. Smith, as the last surviving member of Jackson's
staff, gave the opening prayer in the presence of old comrades and government officials. Leigh Robinson, a wartime
private in the Richmond Howitzers, gave the main address.

Smith had a gentle disposition. People were drawn to
him. He never lost his love for young people. He had a
keen sense of humor. He and Mrs. Smith shared forty-five
years together. She died in October 1916.

For the rest of his life Dr. Smith spent time visiting his
children. When his health failed, he went to live with a
daughter, Mrs. Charles F. Meyers. Her home was in
Greensboro, North Carolina. There at her home, on the
morning of August 6, 1923, at the age of eighty-six years,
"he departed to be with Christ," the last survivor of Stonewall Jackson's staff.

In his memorial, Russell Cecil used Smith's own words:

"I've fought the fight; I've won the race,
I now shall see Him face to face,

197

Who called me to Him long ago
And bade me trust and follow.

The joys of life have been his gift.
My friends I'll find when clouds shall lift;
I'll leave my home and all its store
To dwell with Him forever more."

We started the book with an overview of the expressions and impressions of Jackson's faith as observed by J. William Jones and others. We close with a summary based on remarks of James Power Smith, given at the dedication of the Jackson Memorial Hall in Lexington. Smith said:

> It was Thomas Carlyle who said, "A man's religion is the chief fact with regard to him." And more than of any man of renown of modern times, it is true of Jackson that his religion was the man himself. . . .
>
> Eminent critics are telling us that the campaigns of Jackson will be the study and admiration of military schools for centuries to come. However true that may be, . . . the religion of Stonewall Jackson will be the chief and most effective way into the secret springs of the character and career of this strange man, who as the years go by is rising into the ranks of the great soldier saints of history.[21]

Smith then went on to compare Jackson with Saint Louis of France, Gustavus Adolphus of Sweden, Oliver Cromwell of England, and Gordon of Khartoum.

In those days, speakers started at Genesis and went to Revelation in the same address. Edward Everett did this at Gettysburg, and Hunter McGuire did the same this very day in Lexington, as he shared in the program.

Smith alluded to heredity and genetics. He talked of the influence of Jackson's mother, learning Scripture at her knee, Jackson becoming an orphan and running away from harsh, unloving homes. These events are covered in the biographies of Jackson.

From this bleak childhood came purity, integrity, honesty, and a humble character. Jackson was years ahead of Dr. Norman Vincent Peale, as he came up with the philosophy, "You may be whatever you resolve to be."

Smith traced Jackson's religious pilgrimage. First there was the witness of a dedicated friend at West Point. Next came baptism into the Episcopal Christian faith by an Episcopal priest. Jackson also sought instruction from a Catholic bishop whom he admired. Then came the Lexington years, and visits to the bookshop of John Lyle. The bookstore proprietor introduced him to Dr. William S. White and the rest is history.

With White, Jackson admitted his ignorance of the Christian faith. "He came with entire candor and simplicity to be taught as a little child." Tom spent hours with Dr. White, asking questions, seeking the truth and searching the Scriptures. Smith felt, "The supreme fact in the character of Jackson was that far beyond any man of whom we read, 'God was in all his thoughts.'"

To God Jackson gave his loyalty and devotion. "He acknowledged His supreme authority as the Maker and Redeemer over every part of his being, and every breath of his life, and to that authority he bowed his will implicitly." Perhaps this is the reason he had no fear of death, or falling in battle, everything was placed in God's hands.

Some will argue about his anger and lack of patience. However, Jackson tried to do his best, anything less was poor. What he expected of himself; he expected of others. Perhaps he did not realize that they had not reached the plateau he had achieved. Dr. Stiles said that Jackson came closer to giving God the proper place in life than any man he knew.

His life was filled with simplicity and directness, and he was a humble man. "All things were viewed in the light of the supreme fact of God." This ruled over every aspect of his life.

Jackson "owed all to God, all that he was, all that he had attained, all that he had accomplished, . . . and unto Him belonged all the praise and the glory."

Two strong theological beliefs stand out in the life of Jackson. He believed in "the providence of a personal God." Tom felt God had opened the door for him to go to West Point, protected him during the Mexican War, and that God provided the opportunity for him to go to Lexington. This was the first basis of his fact, and a book could be written about that.

199

Jackson kneeling in prayer at cradle of his infant, Julia.

Jackson at prayer.

Second was Jackson's belief in prayer to the one "whose ears are always open to the cry of His children, and who is ready to hear and answer above all that His children can ask or think." This book has stressed the many moments of Jackson in prayer. He lived a life of prayer.

Although he was curt and demanding with his officers, those close to him stated that they never heard him gossip, or say an unkind remark about anyone.

He sought to share his faith personally. And he did all in his power to get dedicated chaplains into the army, and he worked just as hard to obtain Bibles and tracts for the men, often distributing Christian literature himself. He taught the blacks, he interceded in prayer for his pastor, the folks in Lexington, and his troops.

Yet he enjoyed his faith. He jested with Jeb Stuart, played with the Graham children, and little Janie Corbin at Moss Neck. He shed tears when she died. He was courteous and kind. An English officer said, "[He is] as perfect a gentleman as I have ever known."

Smith then compared Lee and Jackson to two mountain

peaks, different, but standing "on fame's eternal camping-ground, each giving unfading glory to the other."

Smith then concluded his remarks by saying:

> Ten years of faithful toil Jackson gave to the Virginia Military Institute, . . . Through uncounted years to come his great name will rest upon this building as a benediction! The memory of the soldier and his campaigns and victories will abide in this hall, and the spirit of the honest and God-fearing Christian gentleman will come back to speak forever of that fear of God which is the beginning of wisdom, and of that simple and humble faith which is the sure and only way to enduring honor and exaltation.

This was the way James Power Smith, a *preacher Jackson knew*, summarized the great captain's life.

APPENDIX

George W. Junkin

At Spotsylvania Court House, Edward Johnson's division was virtually wiped out. All of the Liberty Hall Volunteers with the exception of two privates and Lieutenant Jones were either killed, wounded or captured. Ted Barclay and the other Confederates who were captured were taken to Fort Delaware.

Among the visitors to the prison, was none other than Dr. George Junkin. He had been living quietly in Philadelphia. Earlier he had ministered to them after Gettysburg.

Dr. Junkin delivered a very powerful sermon. "The services were of a very solemn character." After they were concluded, these college young men all remained to take their old preceptor by the hand. Among the number was a college chaplain; and it was most touching to see the aged man of God throw his arms around the young man's neck and weep, exclaiming, "I never thought you would be engaged in this work!"

As they stood together, Junkin took his old roll book from his pocket and called the roll, sharing what he remembered of each. Then being the diehard Unionist that he was, he showed them how "all had suffered more or less in consequence of their resistance to the best government which God had ever given to men."

He visited the lads again at Fort Delaware on June 11, 1864. He gave out some tracts, and told the story of General Hunter capturing Lexington and burning VMI.

Junkin was back on June 12. He preached morning and evening to a large crowd of Rebel prisoners. "They wore nothing but their drawers and shirts and were barefooted. How strange this must have looked to the doctor. He talked much of Lexington and how much he loved the people and of it being the resting place of his dead wife and daughter. He was much affected, spoke in feeling words of the Liberty Hall Volunteers, how he loved them and how already many had yielded up their young lives for the cause they thought right, while he believed it wrong."

This visit was recorded by Private McCowan in his diary. Junkin had a cane which had been given to him by Jackson. McCowan writes "[Dr. Junkin's] appearance reminds me so much of home. How often have I sat and listened to him in the Presbyterian Church when all was peace."

Dr. James Graham

Long after the Civil War, Mrs. Jackson remarked that the picture taken in Winchester was her favorite. Some feel the picture was taken in the winter of 1862. However, it must have been the autumn of 1862.

The Reverend Mr. Graham was invited to dinner, along with members of the general's staff, at the home of Dr. and Mrs. Hugh McGuire. Mr. Graham was seated "directly opposite to him. . . . He was in perfect health and in fine spirits."

Gettie McGuire, Hunter's little sister, said, "Gen. Jackson, I would like so much to have your picture."

Everyone was surprised by Jackson's reply, "Thank you Miss Gettie, I'll go at once and have it taken."

Despite his aversion to pictures, he did just that. Before the end of the day, some of the other dinner guests were summoned to the studio.

The photographer was Nathaniel Routzahn, originally from Frederick, Maryland, and a man in his early thirties. He had opened his studio in Winchester in 1855.

The Reverend Mr. Graham described earlier the account of the missing button. And he tells us that the picture was taken in late October or early November in 1862.

See Rev. James Graham's memories of Jackson in the book by Mrs. Jackson and Ben Ritter, *Jackson's First War-time Portrait, Civil War Times,* February 1979, pp. 37-39.

Robert L. Dabney

Robert Lewis Dabney was widely recognized as one of the most brilliant, most gifted of Virginia's sons who were living about a century ago. This native of Louisa County exerted an influence that extended throughout the South. One of the most eloquent and popular divines of his troubled generation, he was for thirty years, 1853-83, a professor in Union Theological Seminary. . . . The impact of his theology remained effective long after, in quest of a milder climate, he left the Seminary to teach moral philosophy in the University of Texas. . . .

He consistently reached various audiences through addresses, many . . . books, and countless articles of every kind.

A thoroughgoing conservative in religion, politics, and sociological outlook was Dr. Dabney. By the sheer force of his intellect, the vigorous conviction with which he spoke and wrote, and the eloquence of his expressions, he did much to counteract in the Southern mind the liberalizing influence of Jefferson and Madison. . . .

Herbert G. Bradshaw used these words to describe Dr. Dabney in *The Virginia Cavalcade*, vol. 8, November 1958. The article was "The Preacher Who Designed Four Churches."

Mr. Bradshaw then discussed the Presbyterian Churches designed and built by Dabney: Tinkling Springs in Augusta County; (He wanted the church to be "a very neat, handsome & convenient house, the best country church anywhere in this part of the country"), the Biery Church near Keysville; and the Farmville and College Church at Hampden-Sydney.

Hampden-Sydney College has been in operation since 1776. The College is the tenth oldest institution of higher learning in the United States, and the oldest of the nation's few remaining all-male colleges. The college is affiliated with the Presbyterian Church in the United States.

The 556-acre campus is located seventy miles southwest of Richmond. Farmville, a town of 6,000, is seven miles north. Graduates of this Virginia school was instrumental in starting Princeton Seminary, the University of Virginia, and the Medical College of Virginia was established as the medical department of Hampden-Sydney. As we have seen, Union Theological Seminary was established at the south end of the campus and remained here for seventy-five years before moving to Richmond.

205

Moses Hoge

Dr. Hoge accompanied President Davis and the cabinet when they left Richmond. He did not want to take the oath of allegiance to the United States. Indeed, he felt he could not, so long as the Confederate government existed. In Danville, Hoge shared a room with Secretary Benjamin. Later he shared information with the English writer Lawley who produced a biography on Benjamin. Hoge stayed for awhile at Milton, North Carolina, and then painfully returned to Richmond "to take up the burden of life, with a sad heart, but an unconquered will."

The conditions "were enough to paralyze the strongest heart. . . . Every business was prostrate. Factories were gone. Money had vanished, folks were bankrupt. Bonds were worthless." The people were demoralized. To this situation, the *preachers Jackson knew* had to minister. The stress and strain on the people was as bad as the action on the battlefield.

"But more than all of this, they had lost their independence; their statehood. They were governed as a conquered province." Writing on May 15, 1865, Hoge says, "With every morning light, my sorrow begins a new." He forgot his humiliation in sleep. But then just as in grief, the bereavement hit him afresh each morning." God's dark providence enwraps me like a pall; . . . I cannot explain, but I will not murmur." In September he stated, "Other seas will give up their dead, but my hopes went down into one from which there is no resurrection."

Tucker Lacy

Ted Barclay, a member of the Liberty Hall Volunteers, and a young man who made a profession of faith during the war, kept a journal of his military activities. For April 8, 1864, he writes:

> I heard an elegant sermon from Mr. (Beverly Tucker) Lacy on the text – "Let me fall now into the hand of the Lord." Chron. XXI-13. His style of preaching is just suited to camp and his sermons are generally attended with good results. Yesterday evening he delivered his 'Eulogy on Gen. Jackson'. . . . I suppose there were three thousand persons present, but his address was so good that not one person left the ground until he had finished. It was the most attentive audience I ever saw. And how beautifully and touchingly he held up to our view the character of our dearly beloved General as worthy of imitation, especially as Christians. He just reviewed his early life, his difficulties in acquiring an education, his private life at West Point, his success in his studies, his first experience as a soldier in the Mexican War; next as a private man in the capacity of professor at V.M.I., and member of the church and teacher in the colored Sabbath school in Lexington. Then the great part he had taken in his great struggle for political and religious freedom. . . . He followed him all through his campaigns down to the bloody and dearly bought field of Chancellorsville. He spoke of the revival in the army in '62 and said that he often noticed Gen. Jackson, night after night before retiring, humbly kneeling and imploring the help of God, when he was alone in his tent and knew not that anyone could see him, but his form was reflected through the tent by the light of his candle. He spoke of him as father and husband. His death bed he described so beautifully. . . .

Tucker closed his message by telling about leaving Jackson's bedside, and then seeing the corpse of Frank Paxton, commander of the Stonewall brigade. These two losses made Chancellorsville a double bought field. Lacy appealed "to the old brigade in language which was calculated to move the hardest heart."

This was contained in a letter from Barclay to his mother. After the war, Ted returned to the Lexington area, worked to extend the Valley Railroad from Lexington to Winchester, was co-editor of the *Lexington Gazette,* and was a trustee of Washington and Lee. He died in November of 1915.

James Power Smith

Presbyterian records indicate the following for Joseph Smith: Birth, Fayette County, Pa., July 15, 1796. Jefferson College, 1815; Princeton, 1817-19; Home Missions in Virginia, 1819-21. Ordained Lexington Pres., 1821. Harrisonburg, 1821-26; Staunton, 1826-32. Prof. Frederick Academy, 1832-34, and supply pastor in Frederick the same years. Saint Clairsville, Ohio, 1834-37; President, Franklin College, 1837-38. Pastor, Frederick City, Maryland, 1838-43; President, Frederick College, 1838-44. Pastor, Ellicott's Mills, Maryland, 1844-46. Board of Home Missions, 1846-50. Pastor, Round Hill, Pennsylvania, 1850-55. Greensburg, Pennsylvania, 1856-66. Smith died on December 4, 1868. He was awarded a D.D. degree by Jefferson in 1845, and wrote a history of the college in 1857.

This then is the record of Smith's father.

A letter discovered in recent years and now in place at the Jackson shrine south of Fredericksburg (see page 180) reads:

(see page 180)

Guinea's Depot
12 O'clock   May 9/63

My dear Sister.

Mrs. Hoge & I found the General worse this morning. He had been sinking during the morning but is doing better now the Drs. think.

Mrs. J is very much affected. Mrs. H's arrival is very timeley – and will prove of great consolation to Mrs. Jackson.

I will try to let you know about the Gen. as often as possible.

I am
with much love
your aff. brother
Jas P. Smith

The church in Fredericksburg where Lacy and Smith preached, still has cannon balls in the left front pillar and scars in the walls of the loft and belfry, a witness to the Federal bombardment in 1862. The current bell replaced the one given to the Confederacy to be melted into cannon. The pews of the church were torn loose and converted into resting places for the wounded. And Clara Barton nursed in the church.

Connections

Junkin, White, Lacy, and William Nelson Pendleton are buried in the same cemetery with Jackson in Lexington.

Lacy and Graham served in Winchester. J. P. Smith's mother was from Winchester.

Graham, Hopkins, and Lacy were members of the Winchester Presbytery at one time.

Dabney, Hoge, and J. P. Smith attended Hampden-Sydney; were graduates of Union Theological Seminary.

Lacy and Smith served the Fredericksburg Presbyterian Church.

NOTES

I–J. WILLIAM JONES (Pages 1-21)

1. James I. Robertson, *The Army of Northern Virginia, Memorial Volume.* Dayton, 1976. This is a collection of Memorial Addresses on special occasions after the war. Dr. Robertson, the outstanding teacher and writer from VPI gives a biographical sketch of Jones. Naturally, the Southern Historical Society Papers which Jones edited for a long time, contain much information about the *preacher Jackson knew.* This is a reprint of the work originally done by Jones. Dr. Robertson gives a biographical sketch.
2. *Idem.*
3. J. William Jones, *Christ in Camp: or Religion in Lee's Army* (Richmond, 1888).
4. Jones, p. 13.
5. *Ibid.*, pp. 15-16.
6. *Ibid.*, p. 16.
7. *Ibid.*, p. 20.
8. *Ibid.*, p. 22.
9. *Ibid.*, p. 260.
10. *Ibid.*, p. 250.
11. *Ibid.*, p. 94.
12. *Ibid.*, p. 49.
13. *Ibid.*, p. 82.
14. *Ibid.*, p. 89.
15. *Idem.*
16. Jackson to Anna, July 23, 1861.
17. Richard B. Taylor, *Destruction and Reconstruction,* (New York, 1879) pp. 44-59. This book contains excellent material on Jackson during the days of April and May of 1862 during the middle and the end of the Valley campaign.
18. The Dr. Hunter Holmes McGuire Papers, Richmond, Virginia.
19. Henry Kyd Douglas, *I Rode With Stonewall* (Chapel Hill, N.C., 1940), p. 150.
20. Jones, p. 467.
21. Douglas, p. 197.
22. Robert L. Dabney, *The Life and Campaigns of Lieut-Gen. Thomas J. Jackson* (New York, 1886), p. 715.
23. Jones, p. 96.
24. *Ibid.*, p. 97.
25. *Ibid.*, p. 478.
26. *Ibid.*, p. 481.

II–DR. GEORGE JUNKIN (Pages 22-42)

1. D. X. Junkin, *The Reverend George Junkin, D.D., LL.D. A Historical Biography* (Philadelphia, 1871), p. 12.
2. *Ibid.*, p. 17.
3. *Ibid.*, p. 48.
4. *Ibid.*, p. 50.
5. *Ibid.*, p. 486.
6. *Ibid.*, p. 492.
7. Frank Vandiver, *Mighty Stonewall* (New York, 1957), p. 90.

8. *Ibid.,* p. 98.
9. Junkin, p. 499.
10. *Ibid.,* p. 500. For additional accounts of the Junkin family and their relationship with Jackson, see Margaret Junkin Preston, "Personal Reminiscences of Stonewall Jackson." *Century,* vol. 32, 1886, pp. 927-36.
11. Jackson letter to Laura, April 1854, quoted in Vandiver, p. 101.
12. Junkin, p. 503.
13. Jackson to Maggie Junkin, March 1, 1855, quoted in Vandiver, p. 106.
14. Junkin, p. 502.
15. Junkin, pp. 503-4.
16. Junkin, p. 505.
17. *Ibid.,* p. 515.
18. *Ibid.,* p. 517.
19. *Ibid.,* p. 521.
20. *Ibid.,* p. 524.
21. *Ibid.,* p. 518.
22. *Ibid.,* p. 537.
23. *Idem.*
24. *Ibid.,* p. 541.
25. *Ibid.,* p. 545.
26. *Ibid.,* p. 552.
27. *Ibid.,* p. 553.

III – William S. White (Pages 43-75)

1. W. S. White, *Rev. William S. White, D.D. and His Times, 1800-1873: An Autobiography,* Ed. by his son, Rev. H. M. White, D.D. (Richmond, 1893), p. 22.
2. *Ibid.,* p. 24.
3. *Ibid.,* p. 100.
4. *Ibid.,* p. 102.
5. *Ibid.,* p. 105.
6. *Ibid.,* p. 109.
7. *Ibid.,* p. 111.
8. *Ibid.,* p. 128.
9. *Ibid.,* p. 129.
10. *Ibid.,* p. 130.
11. *Ibid.,* p. 134.
12. *Ibid.,* p. 136.
13. *Idem.*
14. *Ibid.,* p. 138.
15. *Ibid.,* p. 140.
16. Mrs. Jackson, p. 57.
17. *Ibid.,* p. 59.
18. White, p. 142.
19. *Ibid.,* p. 141.
20. *Ibid.,* p. 144.
21. *Ibid.,* p. 147.
22. *Ibid.,* p. 153.
23. *Ibid.,* p. 158.
24. *Ibid.,* p. 159.
25. *Ibid.,* p. 147.
26. Hugh to his father, April 22, 1861, quoted from *Sketches of the Life of Cap-*

tain Hugh White of the Stonewall Brigade by His Father (Columbia, S.C., 1864), p. 42. Cited hereafter as *Sketches.*

27. J. J. White to his wife, Winchester, June 14, 1861. White Letters, University of North Carolina. See also W. G. Bean, *The Liberty Hall Volunteers* (Charlottesville, Va., 1964).

28. Hugh to his sister from Camp Stephens, June 24, 1861; and J. J. White to his wife from Manassas, July 23, 1861.

29. Jackson to Dr. White.

30. White letters.

31. Hugh White to his father, July 23, 1861.

32. Mrs. Jackson, p. 198. The Utterbacks, where Jackson was located, also had a daughter by the name of Penelope. The men in the Liberty Hall Volunteers tried to court her.

33. John Lyle, "Jackson's Guard, the Washington College Company." This is a manuscript at the McCormick Library on the campus of Washington and Lee, Lexington, Va., p. 314.

34. *Ibid.,* p. 315.

35. Hugh to his sister, February 10, 1862.

36. From the diary of Captain Henry R. Morrison of the Liberty Hall Volunteers, March 4, 1862.

37. *Ibid.,* March 23, 1862.

38. White, p. 98.

39. Mary Anna Jackson, "Memoirs of Stonewall Jackson," Louisville, 1895. This was a basic source for the stories about the preachers.

40. Hugh to Henry, near Richmond, early July 1862.

41. White, p. 126.

42. Hugh to his father, August 24, 1862. His last letter home. He went to church this morning, and heard Dr. Joseph C. Stiles preach.

43. White, p. 118. See also Chaplain Hopkins.

44. White, p. 119.

45. White, p. 123. Smith wrote the comments to the *Central Presbyterian.*

46. White, p. 177.

47. *Ibid.,* p. 179.

48. *Ibid.,* p. 174.

49. Mrs. Jackson, p. 463.

50. White, p. 185.

51. *Ibid.,* p. 184.

52. *Ibid.,* p. 187.

53. *Ibid.,* p. 190.

54. *Idem.*

55. *Ibid.,* p. 198.

56. *Ibid.,* p. 208.

57. *Ibid.,* p. 211.

58. *Ibid.,* p. 216.

59. *Ibid.,* p. 219.

60. *Ibid.,* p. 220.

IV – JAMES GRAHAM (Pages 76-89)

1. Some of the letters to and from the Grahams to Jackson are found in the R. L. Dabney Collection at the University of Texas. Mrs. Jackson quotes from them freely in *The Life and Letters of General Thomas J. Jackson* (New York, 1892).

2. James Robert Graham submitted a necrological report of his father to Princeton Theological Seminary, along with a handwritten narrative of his life.

3. See Mrs. Jackson's biography of her husband. Pages 209-39 and pages 355-59 deal much with the Graham-Jackson correspondence.

4. Rev. James Graham, "Reminiscence of General T. J. "Stonewall" Jackson, quoted in Mrs. Jackson's biography, pp. 485-507.

5. Mrs. Jackson, p. 236.

6. *Ibid.*, p. 485.

7. *Ibid.*, p. 488.

8. *Ibid.*, pp. 489-90.

9. *Ibid.*, p. 491.

10. *Ibid.*, p. 492.

11. *Ibid.*, p. 493.

12. *Ibid.*, p. 503.

13. *Ibid.*, p. 504.

14. *Ibid.*, p. 505.

15. *Ibid.*, pp. 500-501.

16. Dr. John Graham wrote a few accounts of his father's wartime experiences. Some of these can be found in Garland B. Quarles, *Occupied Winchester, 1861-1865* (Winchester, 1976). Mr. Quarles, a distinguished educator and historian describes the destruction of the Federal ammunition depot in September of 1862.

17. Cornelia McDonald in her epic work on Winchester during the war, describes Jackson as he looked on that November Sunday in 1862.

18. Ben Ritter, "The Winchester Photography" in *Civil War Times,* (February, 1979).

19. Mrs. Jackson, p. 509.

20. *Idem.*

V – ROBERT LEWIS DABNEY (Pages 90-119)

1. Thomas C. Johnson, *Life and Letters of Dr. Robert Lewis Dabney* (Richmond, 1903) p. 24. This is a key book for anyone interested in a biography of Dabney. The other, of course, is Robert L. Dabney, *Life and Campaigns of Lieut-Gen. Thomas J. Jackson* (New York, 1866). This was the first biography of Jackson to appear. Cited hereafter as *Dabney.*

2. Johnson, p. 3.

3. *Ibid.*, p. 11.

4. *Ibid.*, p. 23.

5. *Ibid.*, p. 27.

6. *Ibid.*, p. 33.

7. *Ibid.*, p. 36.

8. *Ibid.*, p. 39.

9. *Ibid.*, p. 43.

10. *Ibid.*, p. 45.

11. *Ibid.*, p. 47.

12. *Ibid.*, p. 51.

13. *Ibid.*, p. 54.

14. *Ibid.*, p. 56.

15. *Ibid.*, p. 64.

16. *Ibid.*, p. 67.

17. *Ibid.*, p. 68.

18. *Ibid.,* p. 74.
19. *Ibid.,* p. 80.
20. *Ibid.,* p. 81.
21. *Ibid.,* p. 87.
22. *Ibid.,* pp. 96-97.
23. *Ibid.,* p. 95.
24. *Ibid.,* p. 104.
25. *Ibid.,* p. 115.
26. *Ibid.,* p. 116.
27. *Ibid.,* p. 118.
28. White to Dabney, April 4, 1853.
29. Johnson, p. 142.
30. *Ibid.,* p. 144.
31. *Ibid.,* p. 158.
32. *Ibid.,* p. 185.
33. *Ibid.,* p. 210.
34. *Ibid.,* pp. 212-13.
35. *Ibid.,* p. 217.
36. *Ibid.,* p. 261.
37. Jackson to Dabney, April 8, 1862.
38. Hotchkiss Journal.
39. Dabney, p. 264.
40. *Ibid.,* p. 266.
41. Vandiver, p. 292.
42. Dabney, p. 272.
43. Jackson to Dabney, Dec. 5, 1862.
44. Dabney, p. 276.
45. Dabney, p. 282.
46. *Ibid.,* p. 292.
47. *Ibid.,* p. 444.
48. *Ibid.,* p. 461.
49. *Ibid.,* p. 523.

VI – MOSES DRURY HOGE (Pages 120-132)

1. Peyton Harrison Hoge, *Moses Drury Hoge* (Richmond, 1899), p. 3. The name Hoge seems to have been spelled Haig.
2. Hogestown is on U.S. Route 11, between Carlisle and Harrisburg, south of the Susquehanna River. It is near Kingston and the Junkin family home.
3. The Opequon Church is one of the oldest in the Shenandoah Valley. See "The History of the Winchester Presbytery."
4. Earnest Tice Thompson, *A History of Union Theological Seminary in Virginia.* N.d., p. 7.

The Hanover Presbytery, the mother of Southern Presbyterianism, recognized the need of an established seminary within its bounds. A school for liberal education was first. This was Liberty Hall, begun by the Reverend Mr. Graham. This institution became Washington College and then Washington and Lee.

Hampden-Sydney was second, opening its doors on January 1, 1776. The primary concern was to insure a supply of ministers in Virginia and the South.

In 1806, the Hanover Presbytery deplored the lack of religious instruction, and the small number of ministers. They recommended the establishment of a complete theological library for divinity students at Hampden-Sydney College, and too, an attempt to establish a fund to "aid poor and pious youth for the ministry."

By the following spring, twenty-five hundred dollars had been raised, and Rev. Moses Hoge of Shepherdstown came to Hampden-Sydney as president of the theological school. Dr. John Holt Rice became president when Hoge died in 1820.

5. Hoge, p. 21.
6. Hoge, p. 20.
7. Hoge, p. 249.
8. *Ibid.,* p. 254.
9. Jackson, p. 340.
10. James Power Smith, Southern Historical Society Papers, vol. 5, p. 32.
11. Hoge, p. 184.
12. *Ibid.,* p. 275.
13. *Ibid.,* p. 329.
14. *Ibid.,* p. 394.
15. *Ibid.,* p. 397.

VII – ABNER HOPKINS (Pages 133-143)

1. Presbyterian Ministerial Records, Montreat, North Carolina. Courtesy Dr. Ruth See, curator.
2. Jones, p. 465.
3. *Ibid.,* p. 466.
4. *Ibid.,* p. 468.
5. *Idem.*
6. Jones, p. 469.
7. *Idem.*
8. Letter from Hopkins to the widow of E. Franklin Paxton, May 12, 1863.
9. Jones, p. 242.
10. *Ibid.,* p. 243, and also on p. 638.
11. *The Jefferson County Historical Magazine,* vol. 19, p. 42.
12. From the records of the Presbyterian Church, Charles Town, West Virginia.
13. Robert B. Woodward, *A History of the Winchester Presbytery* (Staunton, 1947). See also *Minutes of the Synod of Virginia* (Richmond, 1912), pp. 212-13.

VIII – BEVERLY TUCKER LACY (Pages 144-162)

1. Betts Papers, and the *Central Presbyterian,* November 7, 1900.
2. See Garland Quarles, *The Churches of Winchester* (Winchester, 1976). Woodward, *A History of the Winchester Presbytery* (Staunton, 1947). Presbyterian Records, Montreat, North Carolina.
3. Horace Lacy to Aunt Lizzie Graham, March 20, 1858. Graham Papers, Duke University.
4. Jones, *Christ in Camp,* chapter 9.
5. Jane Howison Beale, c. 1850-1862 an unpublished manuscript now in the museum of the Historic Fredericksburg Foundation.
6. Edward Alvey, Jr., *History of the Presbyterian Church of Fredericksburg, Virginia, 1806-1976,* chap. 4, "The Civil War Years."
7. Mrs. Beale, June 29, 1862.
8. *Ibid.,* Sept. 18, 1862.

9. *Ibid.*, Dec. 13, 1862, and Alvey, pp. 40-41.
10. *Ibid.*, p. 43.
11. Beverly Tucker Lacy, *War Narrative*, R. L. Dabney Collection, Chapel Hill.
12. *Idem.*
13. Sandie Pendleton to his mother, HQS. Second Corps. March 1, 1863, and March 22, 1863.
14. The *Central Presbyterian*, March 12, 1863.
15. Jackson to Dr. White, 1863.
16. Robert Stiles, *Four Years Under Marse Robert* (New York, 1904), p. 139.
17. Jones, p. 230.
18. Lacy, the *Central Presbyterian*, April 7, 1863.
19. Jones, p. 649.
20. Lacy, the *Central Presbyterian*, April 7, 1863.
21. Jones, p. 519.
22. *Ibid.*, p. 522.
23. *Idem.*
24. Lacy to the *Central Presbyterian*, April 7, 1863.
25. George W. Leyden to J. William Jones, Feb. 14, 1869. See Jones, pp. 488-89.
26. Dabney, p. 707.
27. *Ibid.*, pp. 715-24.
28. Ralph Happell, *Jackson* (Richmond, 1971). This booklet, published by the National Park Service, is tremendous. Mr. Happell was historian for many years at Fredericksburg, and has written an account of the last week of Jackson's life in this book.
29. Mrs. Jackson, p. 444.
30. *Ibid.*, p. 453.
31. Jones, p. 484.
32. Mrs. Jackson, p. 457.
33. Jones, p. 523.
34. *Ibid.*, p. 524.
35. *Ibid.*, p. 364.
36. Bean, pp. 179-80.
37. *Central Presbyterian*, November 7, 1900.
38. *Rockbridge County News*, November 8, 1900. Lacy leaves a personal account in the Betts Papers.

IX – JAMES POWER SMITH (Pages 163-201)

1. James P. Smith, "With Stonewall Jackson," *Southern Historical Society Papers* (Richmond, August, 1920), vol. 5, pp. 1-110.
2. The Presbyterian Church in Frederick was established in 1782. In June of 1834, Dr. I. G. Hammer resigned, and from that month until November of 1834, Joseph Smith supplied the pulpit. He then became pastor of the church in July of 1838. Thus he was serving as pastor when James P. was born. Evidently, Mrs. Smith was still at their home in Athens. This comes from the records of the Presbyterian Church in Frederick, and from the papers of the Honorable Eward S. Delapaline of Frederick. James P. Smith also had a link with Winchester. His mother was from that town.
3. Smith, p. 3.
4. *Ibid.*, p. 8.
5. *Idem.*

6. *Ibid.,* p. 10.
7. *Ibid.,* p. 11.
8. Alvey, pp. 107-8.
9. Smith, p. 29.
10. *Ibid.,* p. 35.
11. *Ibid.,* p. 37.
12. *Ibid.,* p. 38.
13. *Ibid.,* p. 44.
14. *Ibid.,* p. 46.
15. *Ibid.,* p. 53.
16. For the accounts of the last week, see Smith, Happell, Mrs. Jackson, and Hunter McGuire.
17. The tribute in Richmond is described in Bean, pp. 120-24; Douglas, pp. 229-31; and Jackson's book, p. 453.
18. Smith, p. 55.
19. *Ibid.,* p. 56.
20. Alvey, pp. 56-61.
21. James P. Smith, address given at the dedication of the Jackson Memorial Hall, Lexington, June 22, 1893.

BIBLIOGRAPHY

Allan, Elizabeth Preston. *Life and Letters of Margaret Junkin Preston*. New New York, 1903.

Alvey, Edward, Jr. *History of the Presbyterian Church of Fredericksburg, Virginia.*

Barclay, A. T. ("Ted") "The Liberty Hall Volunteers from Lexington to Manassas," in Washington and Lee University Historical Papers. No. 6. Lynchburg, Va., 1904.

Bean, W. G. *The Liberty Hall Volunteers*. Charlottesville, Va., 1964.

– – –. "Stonewall Jackson's Jolly Chaplain, Beverly Tucker Lacy," in *West Virginia History*. January 1968.

Dabney, Robert L. *Life and Campaigns of Lieut-Gen Thomas J. Jackson*. New York, 1866.

Happell, Ralph. *Jackson*. Richmond, 1971.

Hoge, Peyton Harrison. *Moses Drury Hoge*. Richmond, 1899.

Jackson, Mary Anna. *Life and Letters of General Thomas J. Jackson*. New York, 1892.

– – –. *Memoirs of "Stonewall" Jackson*. Louisville, 1895.

Johnson, Thomas C. Life and Letters of Dr. Robert Lewis Dabney. Richmond, 1903.

Jones, J. William. *Christ in Camp; Or Religion in Lee's Army*. Richmond, 1888.

– – –. *Army of Northern Virginia: A Memorial Volume*. Dayton, 1976. New edition. Introduction by Dr. James I. Robertson.

Junkin, David X. *The Reverend George Junkin, D.D., LL.D., A Historical Biography*. Philadelphia, 1871.

Paxton, John G. *Memoir and Memorials of Elisha Franklin Paxton, General, C.S.A.* 1905.

Quarles, Garland. *The Churches of Winchester and Occupied Winchester, 1861-1865.*

Smith, James P. "With Stonewall Jackson," Southern Historical Society Papers.

Taylor, Richard. *Destruction and Reconstruction*. New York, 1879.

219

Thompson, Earnest T. *A History of Union Theological Seminary in Virginia.*

Vandiver, Frank. *Mighty Stonewall.* New York, 1957.

White, W. S. *Sketches of the Life of Captain Hugh A. White of the Stonewall Brigade.* Columbia, S.C., 1864.

− − −. *Rev. William S. White, D.D., and His Times, 1800-1873.* Ed. by his son, Rev. H. M. White, D.D. Richmond, 1893.

Woodward, Robert B. *A. History of the Winchester Presbytery.* Staunton, 1947. Graham, Hopkins, Lacy, and Smith had some connection with the presbytery.

Wyndham, Blanton. *The Making of a Downtown Church.* Richmond, 1945. This is the story of Second Presbyterian Church, the one served by Dr. Hoge.

Primary Sources

Jane Howison Beale, "Diary, c. 1850-1862." Fredericksburg, Virginia.

Alexander Betts Papers, with notations by some Second Corps Chaplains. These are contained in manuscript collection No. 3173. University of North Carolina.

The *Central Presbyterian.* Richmond. Full of stories and articles about preachers. The R. L. Dabney Papers. The University of Texas.

The James Graham Letters, included in the Dabney Collection.

Beverly Tucker Lacy. "War Narrative." R. L. Dabney Collection. Chapel Hill.

Minutes of the Presbyterian Church, Fredericksburg, Virginia.

Minutes of the Presbyterian Church, Lexington, Virginia.

Historical Foundation of the Presbyterian and Reformed Churches, Montreat, North Carolina. Files and photographs are kept on all the pastors.

The Pendleton Papers, The University of North Carolina. Chapel Hill.

Princeton Theological Seminary. Princeton, New Jersey. Alumni files.

Union Theological Seminary, Richmond, Virginia. Biographical Sketches of graduates.

Dr. Harry J. Warthern, Jr. Conservation with Dr. James P. Smith during Sunday School days in Richmond.

INDEX

222